The March on Paris

Alexander von Kluck.

The March on Paris

The Memoirs of Alexander von Kluck, 1914

Alexander von Kluck

With Notes by the Historical Section
(Military Branch) of the Committee
of Imperial Defence

Introduction by Mark Pottle

Frontline Books, London

This third impression first published as *The March on Paris and the Battle of the Marne, 1914* in 1923 by Edward Arnold, London

This edition published in 2012 by Frontline Books,

an imprint of
Pen & Sword Books Ltd.,
47 Church Street, Barnsley, S. Yorkshire, S70 2AS.

Visit us at www.frontline-books.com, email info@frontline-books.com or write to us at the above address.

ISBN 978-1-84832-639-2

CIP data records for this title are available from the British Library.

Printed and Bound by the MPG Books Group, UK

Typeset in 11pt Ehrhardt by Mac Style, Beverley, East Yorkshire.

Contents

Introduction by Mark Pottle   vii

Author's Preface   xxvii

Note on Von Kluck's Military Career   xxix

Introductory   xxxi

Chapter 1   Brussels–Antwerp   1

Chapter 2   Brussels–Somme   23

Chapter 3   The Inward Wheel Against the Enemy's Main Forces – Paris – Crossing The Marne   61

Chapter 4   The Battle on the Ourcq   87

Appendix: Order of Battle of the First Army, 1914   127

Bibliography   135

Map of the Advance of the First Army to the Grand Morin & Map of the March of the First Army to the Ourcq and of the Retreat to the Aisne   136

Introduction 'A fighting soldier of the old school': General Alexander von Kluck and *The March on Paris*, by Mark Pottle

eneral Alexander von Kluck's grandly titled *The March on Paris and the Battle of the Marne 1914* follows the progress of the German First Army, of which Kluck was the commander, from its point of assembly at Grevenbroich near Dusseldorf, at the beginning of August, to its resting place on high ground above the Aisne in mid-September. Kluck's army was at the extreme right of the seven that advanced westwards from Germany in 1914, and it formed the fast moving tip of what has been aptly described as a 'great scythe-sweep' through Belgium and northern France.[1] This ambitious manoeuvre, prefigured in the Schlieffen plan of 1905, and central to the thinking of Moltke, the Commander-in-Chief, in 1914, was meant to secure an early victory for Germany in the west, freeing men and materials for what was expected to be a more prolonged war against the Russian 'steamroller' in the east. The emphasis in the west was on speed and manoeuvre, and during its rapid advance First Army covered more than 300 miles in little more than thirty days, travelling a greater distance than any of its more southerly counterparts. It fought major battles against the British at Mons on 23 August, and at Le Cateau on the 26th, and by the 28th was bearing down on Paris from the north-east. That afternoon Kluck's headquarters at Villers Fauçon received a triumphal wireless message from the Kaiser:

---

1. The phase is used by Liddell Hart in his foreword to Gerhard Ritter's *The Schlieffen Plan: Critique of a Myth* (Oswald Wolff, London, 1958), 7.

The First Army is today approaching the heart of France in its victorious march, after winning rapid and decisive victories against the Belgians, the British, and the French. I congratulate the Army on its brilliant successes, and wish to express my imperial gratitude.[2]

Although Kluck's army was subsequently diverted east of Paris, and did not travel to the west, as might have been expected, its advance guards made rapid progress, crossing the Marne on the evening of 2 September. By the 5th they had crossed the Grand Morin, and were effectively south of Paris. This, however, proved to be the furthest extent of their advance. On 9 September First Army began to retreat northwards in the face of Marshal Joffre's decisive counter-offensive. Kluck marched his exhausted troops towards the Aisne, and on 12 September they began entrenching on the plateau on the far side of the river. There, during the ensuing first battle of the Aisne, First Army helped bring to a standstill Joffre's pursuit, laying, in Kluck's own words, 'the foundation stone for the eventual establishment of the German western front from the Aisne to the Yser'.[3]

The March on Paris thus concludes with a description of First Army's march away from the French capital – an irony that eluded Kluck, but which is nevertheless central to his work. The failure to deliver a knock-out blow in the west condemned Germany to what it most feared, war on two fronts, and while all was not lost after the Marne – Kluck himself reported the strategic situation 'by no means unfavourable'[4] – the campaign in the west had assumed an attritional aspect that lengthened appreciably the odds on a German victory. It was inevitable, therefore, that the conduct of the German armies in the west would be closely scrutinized, and particularly those on the right wing where Joffre had successfully counter-attacked. Kluck wrote *The March on Paris* with an eye to future controversy, and with a view to defending his reputation, as well as that of the army that he had been proud to lead.

The book began life as a memorandum drafted by Kluck's highly-rated

---

2. Alexander von Kluck, *The March on Paris and the Battle of the Marne 1914* (Edward Arnold, London, 1920), 75.
3. Kluck, *The March*, 159.
4. Kluck's preface to *The March*, vi (written in Berlin, Feb. 1920).

chief of staff, General-Major von Kuhl, during the winter of 1914/15, when events were still fresh in the memory. It was a factual account, written with the express intention of setting the record straight, and once its historical accuracy had been checked with the senior commanders involved it was circulated:

> ... to certain of the higher leaders for their comments, so that any doubts or contradictory reports as to the work and leading of the First Army might be finally disposed of, and the great achievements of all its corps, its cavalry corps, and their commanders placed definitively in their true light.[5]

The memorandum might have been given no wider circulation had not Kluck's career been effectively ended by shrapnel wounds he received in March 1915. He was placed on half pay, and although there were rumours in March 1917 of a return to active service this did not happen.[6] At some point during his enforced retirement Kluck took up the memorandum drafted by Kuhl and began the process of amplifying it, completing his work in February 1918. *The March on Paris* was thus conceived and completed while the war was still in progress, and although Kluck made use of published works, such as *The Despatches of Sir John French* (London, 1914) and Walther von Kolbe's *Die Marneschlacht* (Bielefeld, 1917), he did not attempt to write a synthesizing, still less a personal, history. Rather, he gave the view from First Army Headquarters, drawing heavily on official records, most notably his own Army Orders, from which he quotes extensively.

The March on Paris is not a descriptive war memoir in the style of so many that appeared after the war. It reveals very little of what Kluck felt and thought: rather, it is a record of what he did – or, more accurately, what he commanded First Army to do. The text marches briskly along, from order to order, and from advance to advance, with scarcely a backwards look. The landscapes through which First Army travelled, and the civilian populations that it encountered along the way, are almost invisible. But

---

5. Kluck, introductory comments to *The March*, 1.
6. *The Times*, 21 October 1916, 7e; 3 March 1917, 5d.

this very narrowness of focus imparts a sense of the drama surrounding the advance, while a clear impression of Kluck's dominant personality also emerges from the pages. He displays throughout a boundless self-confidence, married to a total incapacity to accept defeat. Ground that he was forced to cede in the field he was evidently determined to win back in print.

The book was first published early in 1920 as *Der Marsch auf Paris und die Marneschlacht 1914* by Ernst Siegfried Mittler of Berlin, and on Thursday 20 May an English language edition appeared, published by Edward Arnold, and annotated by the Historical Section of the Committee of Imperial Defence. It was advertised in *The Times* alongside Sir Ian Hamilton's *Gallipoli Diary*, itself destined to become a war classic: they were described as 'contributions of first class importance to the history of the war', and within a few years Kluck's had become recommended reading for officer examinations in the British army.[7] *The March on Paris* appeared in Britain at a time of growing interest in the military history of the war, which was not confined to the works of British authors: 1920 also saw the advent of the military journal *The Army Quarterly*, every issue of which carried an extensive section of 'Notes on Foreign War Books', many of them German. Doubtless because Britain had won the war there was keen interest in the battle experiences of the vanquished enemy, and, as a result of Mons, Le Cateau, and the Marne, Kluck's name was 'probably known to more Englishmen than that of any other German General'.[8] *The Times* capitalised on this familiarity by serialising extracts from *The March on Paris* in three issues just before its publication day.[9]

The most serious charges levelled against Kluck, and from which he sought to defend himself, were, first, that during the advance he travelled east of Paris rather than west, in defiance of the Schlieffen plan, thus exposing his flank to attack on the Marne; and, secondly, that he compounded this error by pushing his forces across the river, 2–4 September, in direct disobedience of the orders of the supreme command (OHL), which wanted him to provide flank protection against Paris. If

---

7. *The Times*, 24 December 1925, 19a.
8. *The Times*, 15 May 1920, 16a–b.
9. *The Times*, 15, 17 and 18 May 1920.

these charges are accepted, then Kluck bears a heavy responsibility for the eventual German defeat on the Marne.

The German armies had travelled east of Paris at the end of August in an attempt to exploit the hitherto obvious weakness of the French left. The manoeuvre is commonly referred to as 'Kluck's turn', and the impression is sometimes given that it was virtually a whim on his part, the implication being that he had a free choice as to whether he went east of the capital or west – as Schlieffen had apparently intended. Quite apart from the fact that Schlieffen's plans were more complex and conditional than this simplification allows – he saw a march west of Paris as a means to an end, and not the end itself – this interpretation places a heavier burden of responsibility on Kluck than is justifiable.[10] As *The March on Paris* makes clear, he had limited freedom of manoeuvre during the advance. Until 27 August he was under Bülow's direct command, and the next evening he received fresh orders from OHL in the form of 'General Directions for the Further Conduct of Operations'. These in fact called for 'an immediate advance of the German Armies on Paris'. First Army was ordered to:

> … march west of the Oise towards the lower Seine. It must be prepared to cooperate in the fighting of the Second Army. It will also be responsible for the protection of the right flank of the Armies, and will take steps to prevent any new enemy concentration in its zone of operations.[11]

Throughout the advance Kluck faced a dilemma that was encapsulated in these orders: he had simultaneously to attack and defend, to probe and protect. When the progress of Second Army was arrested by the French Fifth Army at Guise, on 29 August, Bülow sought support from Kluck,

---

10. For the Schlieffen plan, and the status of Paris in it, see especially: Terence M. Holmes, 'The Reluctant March on Paris: a reply to Terence Zuber's "The Schlieffen Plan Reconsidered"', in *War in History*, 2001 8 (2), 208–32; and Annika Mombauer, 'Of war plans and war guilt: The debate surround the Schlieffen Plan' in *The Journal of Strategic Studies*, October 2005, Vol. 28, No. 5, 857–85.
11. Kluck, *The March*, 76.

who, in accordance with the 'General Directions', changed course to assist him. Instead of travelling west of the Oise, First Army wheeled inwards: the movement was begun on 30 August, and the following morning Kluck received wireless confirmation that it was 'in accordance with the wishes of the Supreme Command'.[12]

Kluck's new alignment suited Moltke's overall purpose. The lack of progress made by the Sixth and Seventh Armies in their attack along the Moselle, on the left wing, had the effect of shortening the overall reach of the German advance. Moltke intended that the armies should henceforth support one another, and close up rather than fan out. The right wing was thus reeled in. Instead of travelling west of Paris in an expansive interpretation of Schlieffen's 'scythe sweep', it passed east, a manoeuvre that was controversial at the time, and which has since become key evidence in any inquiry into the German defeat on the Marne. The French were soon aware that Kluck appeared to be 'sheering off Paris', and when air reconnaissance confirmed this the staff of General Galliéni, military governor of Paris, reputedly cried out 'They offer us their flank. They offer us their flank.'[13] The consequences of this change in direction were momentous, and led to Joffre's decisive counter-offensive on the Marne, but it is nevertheless misleading to trace them all back to 'Kluck's turn', as if he bore sole responsibility. While he of course executed the diversion before Paris, he did so at the behest of Bülow, and in accordance with the wishes of the supreme command. His famous manoeuvre cannot be viewed in isolation: rather, it must be placed in the context of the deployments of the German line as a whole. Contemplating the failure to travel west of the capital Kluck himself later recalled:

Perhaps the deciding factor against it was the belief that, should the offensive be continued on a very broad front, the western wing was not sufficiently strong to crush the French left wing, the British Army, and a possible sortie by the Paris garrison, and at the same time to invest the great fortress-capital.[14]

---

12. Kluck, *The March*, 84.
13. *Army Quarterly*, Vol. XVII, Oct. 1928, 155.
14. Kluck, *The March*, 113.

Evidently, in Kluck's eyes, the right wing was insufficiently strong for the task assigned to it – a repeated refrain in *The March on Paris*. Whether this reflects strategic failings on Moltke's part, or rather the logistical impossibility of the Schlieffen plan, is beyond the scope of this essay to answer. In fairness to Kluck, though, such questions must be raised.

A defence of Kluck against the second charge outlined above – that in attacking across the Marne he disobeyed orders to provide flank protection, inviting Joffre's counter-offensive – is much more difficult to sustain. In turning east of Paris he had satisfied OHL's wishes that the armies on the extreme right work together, but in pressing on independently across the Marne he did just the opposite, contributing significantly to Moltke's difficulties, and to the overall vulnerability of the German right wing.

Once east of the capital at the end of August Kluck forged ahead of Bülow, and during the evening of 2 September IX Corps crossed the Marne after heavy fighting. That night, while he was thus already heavily committed to an advance, Kluck received OHL's order to fall back:

> The intention is to drive the French in a south-easterly direction from Paris. The First Army will follow in echelon behind the Second Army and will be responsible for the flank protection of the Armies.[15]

Bülow's Second Army was then at least a day's march behind, and to the left, of First Army, and rather than mark time waiting for it Kluck decided to continue his advance across the Marne, believing that this fulfilled the spirit, if not the letter, of OHL's instructions. He gave his excuses in a wireless message sent on the morning of 4 September, the essence of which he enlarged upon in a key passage in *The March on Paris*:

> It fell to the First Army to apply the principal pressure in forcing back the enemy, as it was the only force that was immediately on his heels and that could exert the necessary compulsion on his line of retreat. On the other hand, if it halted for two days so as to get in echelon behind the Second Army, the enemy's Higher Command would regain

---

15. Kluck, *The March*, 94.

the complete freedom of action of which it had been deprived. Should the First Army hold back, the great success for which the Supreme Command was confidently striving by 'forcing the enemy in a south-easterly direction' could no longer be hoped for. It was therefore fully in keeping with the spirit of the often-mentioned wireless order for the First Army to continue the pursuit as before across the Marne.[16]

It may be argued that Kluck – 'a fighting soldier of the old school'[17] – was determined to advance in the face of almost any eventuality, and that his logic on this occasion was self-serving: he interpreted the preamble of OHL's message of the night of 2/3 September as an order, and moreover one that conveniently overrode the order that was clearly intended, but with which he did not wish to comply.

That Kluck was disobedient seems incontrovertible, but the Schlieffen plan depended upon the bold action of its commanders, especially those on the right wing, who were responsible for turning the enemy's flank. Kluck was attempting to do exactly this when he was ordered to pause and wait for Bülow on 2/3 September, and the episode highlights again the dilemma that was inherent in his command. He had to protect his own flank, and that of the army inside him, while simultaneously engaging with the enemy, and trying to outflank them. Since he did not have the resources both to attack and to defend he was pulled in two directions. Left to his own devices he clearly preferred to attack. Bülow on his left, however, was more cautious, and lived in constant fear that a gap would open between them, which might lead to their isolation and annihilation. Bülow's concern was shared by OHL, which placed Kluck directly under the former's command during a crucial stage of the advance, 18–27 August, an arrangement reinstituted on 10 September during the retreat.

Kluck resented intensely his subordination to Bülow, although in *The March on Paris* the language is diplomatic. 'The mutual relations between the headquarters of the First and Second Armies', he noted, 'were as helpful as possible'.[18] In reality each baulked at the other's style, and it was

---

16. Kluck, *The March*, 96–7.
17. *The Times*, 20 October 1934, 7a–c.
18. Kluck, *The March*, vi.

surely a mistake to have two such temperamentally different commanders harnessed together on the extreme right. OHL's expedient of placing Kluck under Bülow was never a satisfactory solution: Kluck did not see the wisdom of such temporary subordination, and tried to escape it. He did, however, see the logic of closer coordination between the armies of the right, and argues in *The March on Paris* that it would have been better if the right wing had been placed permanently under a unified command. This would certainly have made coordination between the armies easier and more effective. But it would also have made it more difficult for him to slip the leash, and pursue an independent line – as he was instinctively prone to do.

While Kluck was not blind to the danger to his flank on the Marne, he was not sufficiently aware either. Although Paris and its garrison lay relatively close by he remained untroubled by First Army's exposed deployment in front of it. It is true that in his wireless message of 4 September he had asked OHL for reinforcements, but the impression is that he did so more in order to free up his attack than to shore up his defence: 'The necessary flank protection', he observed, 'weakens the offensive strength of the Army, and immediate reinforcements are therefore urgently needed'.[19] And in spite of requesting reinforcements he did not feel compelled to exercise greater caution. Later in the evening of 4 September he issued further orders for First Army to advance next day towards the Seine, adding: 'If the British can be reached in their retreat they are to be attacked…'.[20] That same evening Joffre issued his own instructions, which show how precarious Kluck's deployments had become. 'The time has come', Joffre observed,

> to profit by the adventurous position of the German First Army and concentrate against that Army all the efforts of the Allied Armies of the extreme left. All dispositions will be made during the 5th September for beginning the attack on the 6th.[21]

---

19. Kluck, *The March*, 99.
20. Kluck, *The March*, 103.
21. James E. Edmonds, *Military Operations, France and Belgium, 1914: Volume I* (3rd edition, 1933), 543.

Joffre had been waiting for an opportunity to attack on his left wing, which he had reinforced especially for the purpose. On 23 August he had available seventeen and a half divisions against the three armies of the German right wing, but by 6 September he could count on forty-one.[22] He thus had the means for a great counter-offensive: with the southwards passage of First Army due east of Paris, in the first week of September, he had the occasion.

The danger to First Army's flank was more readily grasped by Moltke than by Kluck. The former was aware as early as 2 September, from aerial reconnaissance, of a build-up of enemy forces around the French capital, and in the early evening of 4 September he directed First and Second Armies 'to remain facing the eastern front of Paris'.[23] That both armies were now to act as flank protection is an indication of how serious the threat was perceived to be. Kluck received the message early on the 5th, and although he made arrangements for carrying out this order the next day, 6 September, he declined to act at once:

> To carry out the wireless orders of the Supreme Command would mean breaking away from the enemy, and making a two or three days' retreat ... Should the pursuit be stopped, [the enemy] would be able to halt and regain freedom of manoeuvre, as well as an offensive spirit. Taking this into consideration, it seemed preferable first to force him back over the Seine, and to postpone till then the wheeling of the First and Second Armies round to face the eastern front of Paris.[24]

As before, Kluck's offensive spirit carried him into what Joffre identified, with quaint understatement, as an 'adventurous position'. Even when he was informed, on the night of 5 September, that 'very strong enemy forces were being concentrated near Paris to protect the capital and threaten the German right flank' he remained untroubled, believing 'that there was as yet no great danger threatening the right

---

22. Hew Strachan, *The First World War: Volume I: To Arms* (OUP, 2003), 243.
23. Kluck, *The March*, 105.
24. Kluck, *The March*, 105–6.

flank, and that a march back to cover it could be carried out without interruption'.[25]

Later that night Kluck finally became alive to the danger of envelopment, and he then acted quickly and decisively, pulling his forces back across the Marne and throwing them west against Maunoury's Sixth Army during the Battle of the Ourcq. By 8 September his flank was solid, and he was planning a counter-offensive that he believed would turn the tables on the French, enveloping Maunoury's northern wing the next day. Kluck's success in counter-attacking on the Ourcq was impressive, but it came at a price, and one that Bülow was made to pay. On the morning of 7 September Kluck unilaterally recalled III and IX Corps, which had been placed at Bülow's disposal the previous night. This weakened Second Army's right flank, which was obliged to withdraw on the evening of the 8th. When it was further threatened by the advance of the British Expeditionary Force across the Marne the following morning, Bülow had no option but to order a general retreat, even though this widened still further the existing gap between the First and Second Armies – which Kluck later estimated at thirty miles, 'the breadth of front of an Army'.[26]

Into this fraught situation there stepped Lieutenant-Colonel Hentsch, the Commander-in-Chief's emissary, on the last stage of a two-day fact-finding mission that had taken him successively to the headquarters of the five armies of the centre and right. Hentsch spent the night of 8 September at Bülow's headquarters, and his car journey to First Army headquarters the next morning was much delayed by the rapid retreat of the trains and baggage of cavalry divisions across his path. He was therefore fully aware of the difficulty of Bülow's position, and soon became impressed with that of Kluck's also. Just before his arrival, around 11.30 a.m., orders had been issued for the left wing of First Army to pull back, and while Hentsch was discussing the situation with Kuhl news came in of the further advance of the BEF north of the Marne. This seemed to render Second Army's position untenable. For reasons that are not altogether clear Hentsch did not see Kluck himself, but he gave orders to Kuhl instead for First Army to retire, marking with a piece of charcoal on Kuhl's map the approximate

---

25. Kluck, *The March*, 107, 119.
26. Kluck, *The March*, 136.

line that was to be reached. Hentsch was authorised by the commander-in-chief to take such action, and he later cited as his reasons the impending withdrawal of the Second Army, and the withdrawal also of the left wing of the First. In *The March on Paris* Kluck appears to recognise the logic of this position – 'there could be no longer any doubt as to the necessity for the retreat ordered'[27] – but in reality he was never reconciled to it, and unsurprisingly so, for Hentsch was effectively decreeing that the advance was over, and the opportunity lost. As far as Kluck was concerned the outlook on 9 September had been bright:

> A tactical victory of the First Army over the Army of Maunoury on the extreme left wing of the French forces seemed indeed certain, and it was possible that by the continuation of the offensive on the 9th a far-reaching success might have been obtained ...[28]

Kluck's retrospective optimism, however, seems unrealistic, *The Times* observing after the war that 'local successes won at the cost of a great breach between the First and Second Armies could not yield results worth having'.[29] Other British commentators were far less respectful, some dismissing Kluck's 'vapourings' as 'the words of a peace-manoeuvre general who does not understand modern war'.[30] Kluck was doubtless justified in claiming in *The March on Paris* that with the reinforcements later made available on the Aisne the situation on the Marne would have been much different – 'the fortunes of the campaign would have turned very materially in favour of the German right-wing Armies, and transformed the general situation'[31] – but such is the eternal lament of the defeated general.

For post-war German commentators Hentsch was one of the obvious scapegoats for the Marne, and Kluck discreditably contributed to this process. He implies in *The March on Paris* that Hentsch did not take sufficiently into

---

27. Kluck, *The March*, 139.
28. Kluck, *The March*, 139.
29. *The Times*, 18 May 1920, 13a–b.
30. *Army Quarterly*, Vol. V, Oct. 1922, 141; Jan. 1923, 370.
31. Kluck, *The March*, 152, 144.

account the overall strategic impact that a victory on the Ourcq might have had, and in conversation with a British visitor to Berlin after the war he was more blunt: if Hentsch 'had done something to his throat', he said – adding 'not that I would wish it for him' – then 'the whole campaign would have been altered because by then it would have been apparent that no retirement by the Germans was the least bit necessary'.[32] The temptation to blame Hentsch must have been irresistible to Kluck, because it absolved him of all responsibility for the German defeat on the Marne. Not that Kluck accepted that an Allied victory had actually taken place – a contention at once remarkable and highly characteristic, and which was treated with withering scorn in a footnote in *The March on Paris*. The clinching argument in this note is General Franchet D'Espèrey's assessment, given to the troops of his Fifth Army, on the 9th: 'Held on both his flanks, his centre broken, the enemy is now retreating towards east and north by forced marches'.[33] Kluck's inability to accept this scenario, either at the time or subsequently, should not obscure his central role in bringing it about.

The Historical Section's footnotes to *The March on Paris* are especially worth reading. A large proportion of them are devoted to pointing out, with varying degrees of acerbity, and an occasional hint of triumphalism, Kluck's ignorance of the location, strength and deployments of the BEF. He got its position wrong at Mons and Le Cateau, on both occasions running head-on into it, and thus missing the opportunity to outflank it. First Army's persistent and sometimes shocking ignorance about the BEF highlights how little Kluck knew even about what was in front of him. After Le Cateau he believed that he had fought the whole of the British Expeditionary Force, when in fact I. Corps had not taken the field. What undoubtedly contributed to his blindness was his lack of access to cavalry and air reconnaissance. As *The March on Paris* makes clear, he was denied the services of von Marwitz's cavalry corps at key moments during the advance, partly at Bülow's instigation. In consequence he prescribed a series of zigzags after leaving Belgium that never properly tracked the movements of the BEF during its tortuous retreat south to the Marne.

---

32. Violet Bonham Carter, *Champion Redoubtable* (Wiedenfeld & Nicolson, London, 1998), 142.
33. Kluck, *The March*, 145n.

The combined failings of German intelligence, communication, and command, all offer a more credible defence for Kluck's actions on the Marne than the scapegoating of the hapless Hentsch. Kluck claimed that if he had known about the difficulties experienced by the German armies on the left wing he would never have pressed forward on the right as he did:

> The First Army Commander was quite unaware of the all-important fact that the Fourth, Sixth, and Seventh Armies were being held up east of the Moselle, and thus allowing the enemy there freedom of manoeuvre. Had this been known in time, the idea of crossing the Marne with any large forces of the First Army would not have been entertained![34]

While this explanation exhibits an obvious desire on Kluck's part retrospectively to defend himself, his message to OHL on the morning of 4 September does prove that he had contemporary concerns on this point:

> The First Army requests to be informed of the situation of the other Armies, whose reports of decisive victories have so far been frequently followed by appeals for support ... Owing to the ever-changing situation, it will not be possible for the commander of the First Army to make any further important decisions unless he is kept continuously informed of the situation of the other armies who are apparently not so far advanced.[35]

This may represent no more than an attempt on Kluck's part to blame OHL for failing to keep him informed, and thus pre-empt any criticism for his disobeying the order of 2/3 September. But, as he implies in *The March on Paris*, it was unrealistic of OHL to seek to drive the enemy south-east from Paris without first knowing the strength of the enemy forces arrayed there. This places the burden of responsibility for the Marne with OHL, and Moltke, but the latter too was deprived of

---

34. Kluck, *The March*, 112.
35. Kluck, *The March*, 99.

information at key times. He received no important news from his armies for three days of the battle of the Marne, 7–9 September inclusive, and Falkenhayn observed:

> When the General Staff told me this morning early [the 9th] that no information of any kind had come from the front, I went to Moltke, as it appeared to me to be incredible. But the incredible is true. Since early yesterday Moltke has only received one message from the five Armies on the right. And that was from Lieutenant-Colonel Hentsch ...[36]

It speaks volumes that, at a crucial stage in the advance, when events were fast-moving, Moltke dispatched Hentsch by motor car on a protracted tour of five army headquarters simply to get a clearer idea of what was going on.

The German failures in communication, to which Kluck amply attests, stemmed from inadequate pre-war planning. He observed that 'the means of communication between the First Army and those in supreme command were totally inadequate', and that messages from OHL sometimes 'did not arrive till after the most important events had already begun'.[37] He also encountered serious problems of supply, which were intensified the further that the front moved from Germany. First Army arrived in France under-strength and under-equipped, and Kluck had to order his troops 'to take the utmost care to husband their ammunition and to make a special point of picking up any left on the battlefields'.[38] Without absolving the German military of responsibility for waging a war of aggression in the west, *The March on Paris* does help to dispel the myth of a supremely efficient German military machine, marching with precision to the beat of Schlieffen's drum, and foiled only by the failings of commanders who proved unequal to the task. It reveals the immense problems – not least logistical – of waging war on this unprecedented scale, and it adds to a sense of the recklessness of the German gamble in 1914.

Notwithstanding the many difficulties that were not of his own making,

---

36. *Army Quarterly*, Vol. XII, April 1926, 148.
37. Kluck, *The March*, 109.
38. Kluck, *The March*, 70.

Kluck's generalship was far from being faultless during the advance. He quotes with approval an Athenian maxim that the greatest commander is 'he who knows best what is going on behind the enemy's lines', yet, for the reasons discussed above, he was often unclear where these lines were, let alone what was going on behind them. In the absence of hard intelligence he tended to treat as certainties assumptions that often proved baseless, and in consequence his adversaries eluded him. The Belgians, he wrote, 'have always managed to escape our grasp, so that their Army has not been decisively beaten nor forced away from Antwerp', while the British 'escaped the repeated attempts to envelop them',[39] and when all of his excuses have been made, the fact remains that Kluck failed to fix and annihilate either of these armies. Most difficult of all to understand, given his push and thrust on the Marne, and his dynamic response on the Ourcq, is his failure to press home his undoubted advantage over Smith-Dorrien's forces during and directly after the Battle of Le Cateau on 26 August. Had he done this he might have destroyed more than half of the BEF, leaving the remnants in a desperate state, but he let the opportunity slip: while his troops rested the British marched through the night, opening a gap that was never seriously closed. It is worth remembering, though, how tired Kluck's troops must have been even by this point. An officer who served with Second Army reported that when they reached the Marne over a week later they were exhausted, and he quotes one soldier as saying: 'The French needn't be frightened of us any more; we have been marched *kaput*.'[40]

The March on Paris is the memoir of a professional soldier, couched in a military idiom, and concerned with his side's fight 'against enemies worthy of their steel'.[41] And, as has already been noted, its horizons generally extend no further than the battlefield. First Army fought across great swathes of Belgian and French countryside, and yet the civilian inhabitants are almost never mentioned. When his headquarters moved near Solesmes on 25 August, the eve of Le Cateau, 'The French peasants

---

39. Kluck, *The March*, 32, 78.
40. *Army Quarterly*, vol. XIII, Jan. 1927, 405.
41. Kluck, *The March*, 168.

were terrified, but became somewhat reassured later'.[42] It is a rare glimpse of the fear that must have been engendered by the presence of the invader. The glaring exception to this invisibility concerns the unfortunate Belgians who were killed in order to deter a guerrilla-style resistance in their homeland. Kluck is bluffly matter-of-fact about the punishments meted out by troops who had 'suffered by treacherous acts on the part of the population, apparently instigated thereto by the local authorities'.[43] At Louvain, later the scene of one of the worst German atrocities of the war, First Army discovered the 'corpses of women with rifles in their hands, killed during the fighting':

> Proclamations warning and threatening the population had no effect, so that a severe and inexorable system of reprisals had to be applied by the commanders on the spot, to put an end to this state of things. Punishments under martial law, the shooting of individuals, and the burning of houses, became numerous along and behind the front, but were slow in remedying the evil … These evil practices on the part of the population ate into the very vitals of the Army until the southern frontier of Belgium was reached.[44]

The latter sentence was undoubtedly an exaggeration, and elsewhere Kluck observes that the advance was 'not actually delayed' by such resistance.[45] And while he gives the impression in *The March on Paris* that there was a semblance of order to the reprisals that were carried out in Belgium, an interview with a correspondent of the *Chicago Daily News* in October 1915 suggests a very different picture:

> Barbarities are impossible to prevent in war. Any large army is bound to have ruffians. Though cases are less frequent now than they were in Belgium, instances do occur – some French, some British. These stir up a fury in the troops which makes them hard to control. It was so in

---

42. Kluck, *The March*, 60.
43. Kluck, *The March*, 25.
44. Kluck, *The March*, 29, 26.
45. Kluck, *The March*, 32.

Belgium. Our men did not mind being shot by rifles or cannon, but they were infuriated when struck down by women through treachery. When such things occur then war becomes cruel and soldiers become impossible to control. The Belgian campaign in all its phases will never be known. Much has got into the papers, but not all.[46]

This interview was reprinted in *The Times*, and must have fuelled British outrage at German 'frightfulness' – the contemporary Anglicisation of the German *schrecklichkeit*, the policy of creating terror, and thus quiescence, in a civilian population. It is possible to read *The March on Paris* as if it described nothing more than a gigantic war game, so little is there about the human cost involved. But Kluck was of course not exceptional in this respect: rather, he was typical of his class, and it was the prevalence of this outlook in Wilhelmine Germany that made possible the wholesale invasion of neutral Belgium in August 1914.

It is tempting to imagine Kluck despondent after the war, a broken man. In January 1915 the elder of his two sons was killed at Ostend, serving with the Marine Corps, and on the same day that Kluck was himself wounded his younger son was badly injured in a motor accident. His own wounds of course led to the untimely end of his career, and he watched from the sidelines the defeat of Germany, and the punitive Versailles settlement that followed. But according to the testimony of several British visitors who saw him in Berlin, some at the height of the Ruhr crisis, Kluck was oppressed neither by the present nor the past. Violet Bonham Carter, who met him in March 1923, found him 'perfectly charming' company: 'Though 77 he didn't look a day older than 64. He was a vigorous and unconventional talker with a first rate sense of humour – and a great gift of words. One felt *tremendous* vitality and energy about him and no military rigidity or conventionality.'[47] To this interlocutor, who spoke reasonably good German, he described his frustration with Hentsch, and his belief that no retirement from the Marne had been necessary. Another British visitor – a representative to the disarmament commission – spent two

---

46. *The Times*, 19 October 1915, 7c.

47. Violet Bonham Carter, *Champion Redoubtable* (Wiedenfeld & Nicolson, 1998), 142.

hours talking with Kluck, and later recalled that he took 'unconcealed pleasure' in learning that he was the 'eponymous hero of a marching song of the old BEF – untranslatable in more senses than one'. 'Kaiser Bill' was sung to the tune of 'Pop goes the Weasel':

> Kaiser Bill is feeling ill,
> The Crown Prince, he's gone barmy.
> We don't give a cluck for old von Fluck
> And all his bleeding army.

'Old von Fluck' was, for his part, more than generous towards the BEF, the quality of which he said had astonished his side in 1914. It was, he said, incomparable: '*Unvergleichlich! Unvergleichlich!*'[48] But if Kluck was not broken by his experiences in the war, he was certainly consumed by them. According to Helen D'Abernon, the wife of the British Ambassador in Berlin: 'The General can only discourse in his native tongue and his one and only topic is the 1914 advance'.[49]

---

48. J. H. Morgan to the Editor: *The Times*, 8 August 1928, 13e.
49. Helen D'Abernon, *Red Cross and British Embassy* (1946), 104.

Author's Preface

The following review of events was completed on the 6th February, 1918. The books which have since been published on the period dealt with, such as Major Bircher's valuable contribution on the Battle of the Marne, that of Field-Marshal French (which appeared in the summer of 1919), and General Maurice's 'Forty Days in 1914,' have not been taken into account. The temptation to enter into the controversies raised by General Baumgarten-Crusius's work has been avoided, although it undoubtedly contains facts of great importance; so also with the books of Field-Marshal von Bülow and General von Hausen. Only opinions formed at the time are recorded; those arrived at later have been omitted.

These limitations seem most necessary in order that the appreciation of the situation as it appeared to the headquarters of the First Army in 1914 may be recorded, unaffected by other influences. With this in view, the more important orders and documents have been reproduced verbatim in the text.

The point of view of the Army Commander as regards the dangers of a crossing of the Marne at the beginning of September, 1914, is set forth in the third part of this review. Major-General v. Nordenswan, a Swede, has made many apposite remarks in his book 'Strategisches aus dem Weltkriege,' and has developed them as much as the information at his disposal allowed.

The mutual relations between the headquarters of the First and Second Armies were as helpful as possible. Where opinions differed each stood by its own, and it is for future historians to inquire which party had the greater reason on its side. The general situation after the necessary 'regrouping' of the German Western Army seemed by no means unfavourable, inasmuch as the political and strategic objectives of the war became limited to taking the greatest possible advantage of the strategic weakness of the enemy. To discover where this lies is the principal duty of the supreme command in war.

Von Kluck,
Generaloberst
Berlin, February, 1920

Note on Von Kluck's Military Career

Alexander von Kluck was born on 20th May, 1846, at Münster in Westphalia, and was therefore two months younger than his rival, von Bülow. His father was a Government architect. He joined the 55th Infantry Regiment on 13th October, 1865, and a few months later took part in the Main Campaign of the war of 1866 as *Fähnrich* (probationary officer). He was promoted Second Lieutenant on 16th August, 1866. In this rank he served in the Franco-German War, and was wounded in the arm and body at the Battle of Colombey-Nouilly on the east side of Metz on 14th August, 1870, receiving the Iron Cross, 2nd Class. He was promoted Lieutenant in October, 1873, and married Baroness Fanny von Donop a year later. He became Captain in 1878, Major in 1887, Lieutenant-Colonel in 1893, commanding in the last rank an Infantry N.C.O. School for some time. In 1896 he was ennobled by the Kaiser, and given command of *Landwehr* District No. 1 Berlin. He was promoted Colonel in 1896, given command of the 24th Fusilier Regiment, and shortly afterwards promoted Major-General and made Commander of the 23rd Infantry Brigade. His next step to Lieutenant-General and Commander of the 37th Division came in April, 1902. He remained in this position four years, when he was advanced to General and the command of the V Army Corps. On 1st October, 1913, he was made an Army Inspector, and on 27th January, 1914, promoted to the rank of *Generaloberst*.

It will be observed that, unlike von Bülow, he had no Staff service, and practically his whole career was spent with troops. On outbreak of war he was appointed Commander of the First Army. Early in 1915 he was, after being wounded, it is believed, relieved of his command and not re-employed in the field.

Introductory

T he following reflections are based on the daily notes of the Army Commander, the official documents, and other sources mentioned in the Bibliography. Their object, so far as the provisional state of historical investigation permits, is to explain and supplement the books and pamphlets already published. Of these, the first volume of Stegemann's history frequently unveils the secret motives of the higher command with striking perspicacity, and skilfully brings out the strategic coherence of the operations.

They are founded on a Memorandum by the commander of the First Army, the original of which was drafted by the Chief of the Staff. It was written during the position warfare on the Aisne in the winter months of 1914–1915, whilst the main events were still vivid in the memories of all those who had taken part in them. This Memorandum was completed and circulated to certain of the higher leaders for their comments, so that any doubts or contradictory reports as to the work and leading of the First Army might be finally disposed of, and the great achievements of all its corps, its cavalry corps, and their commanders placed definitively in their true light.

For the purpose of this Memorandum, the campaign was divided up into sections – Brussels, the Somme, the Grand Morin, the Ourcq, and the Aisne. Such a division seems suitable, and this review of those great times will practically conform to it.

The stage which historical research has reached up to that time (about April, 1915) is shown by the introduction to the Memorandum, which is therefore quoted verbatim:

'This account of the operations of the First Army from the beginning of the advance until the position along the Aisne was occupied is based entirely on the records of Army Headquarters. It was possible to give an unbiased description of each situation, as it appeared to Army

Headquarters, from the intelligence and operation reports in their possession at the time and in the light of which their decisions were formed. It was, however, not possible to consider and criticize these in their connection with the general situation as a whole; neither could the fighting of each corps be described by any means without bias in this respect, nor the results adequately appreciated. To do this it would have been necessary to examine the records of the neighbouring armies and of Great Headquarters, as also those of corps and divisions, which were not available at Army Headquarters. The historical accuracy of the account given in this Memorandum has been concurred in by the corps commanders of the First Army, or, if they were not available, by General Staff officers of their staff.'

The time now seems to have arrived to review the sources of information already available, in order to amplify them from the point of view of the commander, and to exhibit the documents, orders, and appreciations put aside at an earlier period owing to lack of time and space, and to place in a clearer light the events which took place on the western flank of the German Armies during August and September, 1914. At the same time, the Memorandum will gain imperishable value as a guide to assist in following the forward rush of the German Armies. A calm survey of the events is all the easier now that three years have elapsed since they took place.

Chapter One

Brussels–Antwerp

On the 2nd August, 1914, the first conference of the commander of the First Army with Generalmajor von Kuhl took place. The latter had been appointed his Chief of the Staff; he was formerly employed as Quartermaster-General in the 'western section' of the Great General Staff at Berlin. He left the same day for Stettin, which was the place of assembly for First Army Headquarters, and the Army Commander followed the next day. On the 4th August the preliminary conferences between the Chief of the Staff and the Deputy Chief of the Staff with regard to the general work of the First Army Staff were concluded with complete unanimity. As the right flank of the German Armies in the west, the First Army had a most important part to play in the execution of a wide movement, probably of an enormous wheel through Belgium and Artois and perhaps into Picardy. It was evident that large tracts of country would have to be traversed with heavy fighting, and that many obstacles would have to be overcome. Rapidity of movement would be the primary condition of success in attaining the ultimate objective, which was to disperse first the Belgian Army, then the British Expeditionary Force, and finally to fall on the French Armies.

At the outset the order of battle of the First Army included the II, III, and IV Corps, the III and IV Reserve Corps, and the 10th, 11th, and 27th *Landwehr* Brigades; the IX Corps was assigned to it shortly afterwards. There was no heavy artillery with the two Reserve Corps, and their establishment of machine-gun companies was most inadequate: the III Reserve Corps had seven and the IV Reserve Corps only four. The total strength of the First Army at that time was 142 battalions of infantry, 32 squadrons of cavalry, 110 batteries of artillery, and 21 pioneer companies. The important auxiliary units, such as ammunition columns, and the medical, supply, and communication troops, were quickly placed on a war footing. Under the able direction of the Chief of the Staff and his

Deputy and of the Chiefs of the Medical and Supply Services, the task of forming the different Staffs, organizing their duties, and inculcating the spirit in which these would be carried out, went quietly forward; zeal and enthusiasm, already intense and glowing, were raised to the highest pitch.

By the evening of the 7th August the Staff of the Army was ready to leave Stettin by rail for Grevenbroich. The rail transport of the troops for the Western front was carried out with a remarkable punctuality. The civilian population and the troops vied with one another in patriotic demonstrations, and the food given to the troops by the population and by the indefatigable Red Cross workers considerably exceeded their needs.

The Staff settled down to hard work and an uninterrupted life of conferences, important decisions, and examination of intelligence; recreation was cut down to an absolute minimum. The composition of the Staff seemed a most happy one, and an eventful future proved that it was so. The Chief of the Staff of the First Army, Generalmajor von Kuhl, was a notable man, of most energetic character and wide views. Mentally and physically he was imperturbable, and, in addition to an extremely cultivated mind, he possessed a personal bravery on the battlefield which from time to time evoked a caution from the Army Commander.

Colonel von Bergmann, the Deputy Chief, who displayed an equal indifference to danger, and had an inexhaustible capacity for work, was conspicuous as a most careful guardian of that vital factor in the life of an army, the collective system of supply, ammunition replenishment, lines of communication work, and transport generally, besides being a sturdy protector of the interests of those services at Headquarters.

Colonel von Berendt, in his capacity as General commanding the artillery, gained the highest credit by the manner in which his arm of the service was employed in all the important fighting, both in open and in position warfare; he showed an exemplary personal bravery in all the battles and minor actions. To skilful use of his artillery were due some of the most brilliant successes in France, on the Vistula, on the Danube, in the Balkans, and in Northern Italy. It was his lot to take part in the most critical of the great struggles of the war.

Generalleutnant Telle was already well known to the Army Commander, both by his participation in the siege manoeuvres at Posen in 1907 and as commander of the pioneers in the First Army Corps district, where his intelligent and conscientious work in many capacities had shown to the greatest advantage. Extremely active day and night and always looking ahead, it was due to him that, to the farthest bounds of his wide sphere of action, obstacles and hindrances were cleared away and blunders put right, no less in the period of open than in that of trench warfare, thus ensuring the primary conditions of carrying on a war of movement with large masses. In trench warfare his insight and energy inspired the unselfish labours of the famous pioneers of the First Army.

In addition to the above must be mentioned with gratitude and praise the Army Commissary Litty, whose early death was a severe loss to the Administrative Staff of the Army, and the Director of Medical Services, Dr Thel, whose wholehearted devotion to the medical arrangements is worthy of the greatest credit.

With an Army Staff so admirably suited to their work, the varying fortunes of the war could be faced with the utmost confidence. All its members were men of earnestness and strong will. Their chiefs kept in mind the words of Moltke: 'If one considers how small an amount of success is due to one's individual self, and through what weak instruments God manifests His greatness, it is a simple matter to be modest.' The immortal master of the art of war goes on to ascribe the chief credit for a successful undertaking to 'the brave troops who know how to win victory wherever one sends them.'

As the result of experience in peace and war during a long life and forty years' study of military history, the Army Commander set down a few reflections which were communicated to corps headquarters:

'The governing factors of rapid and successful warfare are thoroughly war-trained, disciplined troops and the full employment of all available *time*. Hence we obtain speed without haste in leaders of all ranks, and that fostering of innate bravery which is the greatest of all assets. During the deployment of the Army and the times, so pregnant with consequences, that will follow it, every spare hour, every spare minute, should be and must be consistently devoted to maintaining and increasing the *fighting qualities* of the troops. Practice in the use of their weapons in quarters, bivouacs, or wherever it may be, both before and in the intervals of active warfare, will help those men whose training has been unavoidably interrupted to full proficiency in their effective use. This applies to all fighting units, to the *Landwehr,* and to the lines of communication and *Train* troops. If carried out in the right spirit and not overdone, it will increase the man's self-confidence and so *strengthen his moral courage.* This is the foundation of fighting efficiency. Every achievement within human possibility is practicable in war provided the subordinate commanders keep one single object in view – namely, *success by efficiency against superior numbers.* It is a grave mistake to regard a reported fighting inferiority of one's opponents as a necessary preliminary to victory. It is the cause of missing many an opportunity and of spoiling the chances of obtaining a rapid though difficult success, when every atom of strength ought to be put into the fight.

'There are countless ways of raising and maintaining the fighting power of an army. They depend on the character and energy of its leaders. Thus particular attention must be paid to keeping the marching capacity of the men at the highest pitch, by guarding against the many insidious influences that may affect it, especially sore feet and other internal and external injuries caused by long marches, ill-fitting boots, etc. Again, a constant watch should be kept over the supply of food and ammunition and over the medical care of all ranks, including the Army Staff. Neglect of any of these matters will diminish the fighting strength of the Army. All wastage of man-power must be jealously guarded against, as every possible rifle must be available at the decisive moment of the operations. In our present military situation, this is a matter of hard and absolute necessity.'

Four points of tactical interest were also added to these notes as worthy of attention. It was hoped that instructions on these lines issued by corps commanders would tend to divert the overflowing and light-hearted enthusiasm of the troops to a consideration of the full seriousness of the days before them.

The first important Army Order was drafted during the forty-nine-hour railway journey from Stettin to Grevenbroich, and issued on the 10th August, after arrival in the concentration area:

'The First Army will deploy on the extreme right wing of the Armies. As soon as the assembly in the concentration area is completed, the Army will be closed towards Aix-la-Chapelle, and, avoiding Dutch territory, will hold itself in readiness on the roads north of Liège leading across the Meuse between Visé and Herstal. The movement of the Army on Aix-la-Chapelle and its passage across the Meuse must be carried out rapidly.

The concentration in a very narrow area and the length of the columns during the advance will need careful organization and preparation. Great demands will be made on the marching power of the troops.'

This order was based on the following instructions for the deployment issued by the Supreme Command (O.H.L.): 'The main forces of the German Army are to advance through Belgium and Luxemburg into France. Their advance is to be regarded as a wheel pivoting on the area Thionville–Metz. Should Belgium offer resistance to the advance through its territory, Liège is to be taken by the Second Army, so as to free the main roads which are covered by that fortress. For this purpose the 11th Infantry Brigade of the III Corps and the 14th Infantry Brigade of the IV Corps (First Army) have been placed under the orders of the General commanding the X Corps. As soon as the IX Corps, temporarily allotted to the Second Army, has moved forward, the First Army is to advance towards Aix-la-Chapelle. When Liège has been taken and as soon as the First and Second Armies are in position on the roads of advance level with Liège, the general advance of the main forces will be ordered by the Supreme Command.

'The Second Army will march with its right flank on Wavre, and the First Army will receive orders to march on Brussels and to cover the right flank of the Armies. Its advance, together with that of the Second Army, will regulate the pace of the general wheel.'

The II Cavalry Corps,[1] consisting of the 2nd, 4th, and 9th Cavalry Divisions, was at first placed under the Second Army; when the advance began it was to be under the immediate orders of the Supreme Command and advance north of Namur towards the line Antwerp–Brussels–Charleroi, in order to discover the position of the Belgian Army, to watch for any landing of British troops and for the arrival of French forces in Northern Belgium. It was also to keep First Army Headquarters supplied with information.

Meanwhile, between the 7th and 15th August, the assembly of the First Army on the left bank of the Rhine north-east of Aix-la-Chapelle, with its main base at Düsseldorf, was being completed without hindrance.

---

1. Höhere Kavallerie Korps (H.K.K.) II. It waa under the command of General von der Marwitz.

The situation on the arrival of Army Headquarters at Grevenbroich on the evening of the 9th August was as follows: General Emmich had occupied Liège with three brigades, after capturing Fort Barchon (five miles north-east of Liège, and on the right bank of the Meuse near the southernmost of the roads leading westwards between the Dutch frontier and the fortress). The bombardment of the other forts was probably to begin on the 10th August. The bridge of Visé had been destroyed. French as well as Belgian troops had been reported in Brussels, although the French II Corps, to which they were said to belong, was discovered on the 9th in the Thionville district. British troops were expected to disembark at Zeebrugge. The detrainment of the fighting troops of the First Army would be completed as follows: Those of the III and IV Corps by the 11th, II Corps by the 12th, III Reserve Corps by the 13th, and IV Reserve Corps by the 14th. The 14th August was regarded as the probable date for the advance through Aix-la-Chapelle.

On the 10th the situation became clearer. The 2nd and 4th Cavalry Divisions, advancing through St. Trond, drove a part of the Belgian Cavalry Division back on Tirlemont. Enemy's cavalry had also been seen at Diest, thirty miles south-east of Antwerp. The 9th Cavalry Division of General von der Marwitz's Cavalry Corps failed to cross the Meuse between Liège and Huy, though north of Liège detachments of the IX Corps had crossed the river. The restoration of the bridge at Visé was not practicable, as it was under fire from Fort Pontisse, and so another bridge was constructed by the X Corps farther north at Lixhe. The bridge at Argenteau had been destroyed and that at Herstal was in our possession. The uncertain situation about Liège prevented the issue of any definite orders, besides which the roads, which had been torn up and blocked, needed a great deal of repair. The only preparations that could be made were those for the difficult march through Aix-la-Chapelle. At 9 p.m. the following Order arrived from the Supreme Command: 'The march of the First Army to its position of deployment abreast of Liège by the roads mentioned in the deployment orders will begin at once. The IX Corps will still be under the orders of the commander of the Second Army. On the arrival of the First Army this corps will clear its front.'

The 13th August was therefore fixed as the date for the march through Aix-la-Chapelle instead of the 10th, and the necessary movements were ordered preparatory to the advance of the corps. Their leading brigades were to reach their following destinations: The II Corps, Herzogenrath; the IV Corps, Birk; and the III Corps, Weiden. The detrainment of the III Reserve and IV Reserve Corps could then take place at stations in advance of the present concentration area, and they would follow the other corps as soon as ready, and with at least a day's march interval.

On this same day, the 10th August, the important instructions for the march through Aix-la-Chapelle were issued: 'The march through the town will, so far as can be foreseen, take place by three roads: the II Corps and III Reserve Corps by the road Herzogenrath–Richterich–western side of Aix-la-Chapelle–F. Adams's inn–hill 341 (General Staff map)–Gemmenich; the IV Corps and IV Reserve Corps by the road Birk–west of Euchen–Wurselen–through the centre of Aix-la-Chapelle–(Prussian) Moresnet; and the IX and III Corps by the road Weiden–Haaren–eastem side of Aix-la-Chapelle–Eynatten. [A sketch-map of the routes to be followed accompanied these instructions.] Major-General von Stumpff, the Commandant of Aix-la-Chapelle, will mark the line of these roads through the town, avoiding any mention of what corps are to use them, and will block the side-roads; he will send a sketch of the road sections allotted to each of the corps as soon as the order for the advance is given. He will also ensure that the march through the town proceeds smoothly and without interruption, and that the troops use no other roads than those allotted to them. The troops themselves will be ordered to carry out any instructions that he may give; any disorder is to be immediately suppressed with the utmost rigour. The well-ordered execution of the march through Aix-la-Chapelle is a preliminary essential for the success of the movement of the Army across the Meuse, which will take place immediately afterwards'

At the outset of the operations, it was of the utmost importance that no time should be lost. Directions were attached to these instructions detailing officers and troops to assist the Town-Commandant and forbidding billeting in the town, except for the highest Staffs, and for arrangement for keeping up communication with the Second Army and with the IX Corps, as well as an estimate of the probable duration of the march through the town, which would take several days. Taking into account the careful preparations by corps headquarters and the march-discipline of first-class troops, everything seemed arranged for the movement of over 200,000 troops with all their baggage through the defile formed by a town only 2,000 yards in breadth. The time of starting for the march and the corps' destinations beyond the town were not stated.

On the 11th August the situation around Liège appeared unchanged. The commander of the Second Army considered that there was not sufficient heavy artillery, and so no one could say how long it might be before the northern forts were captured. Moreover, before they had fallen, it was impossible for the IX Corps to clear the roads between Aix-la-Chapelle and the Meuse, or for the advance north of Liège to begin. Nevertheless, the Supreme Command took a more cheerful view of the situation, as was shown by its order quoted above for rapid preparations to be made for the advance. From information received up to the evening of the 11th August, the Belgian Army appeared to be deployed on the front Antwerp–Louvain–Namur. The II Cavalry Corps was still about St. Trond, with its 9th Cavalry Division south-west of Liège. The I Cavalry Corps was marching on Dinant.

Although the general idea of the initial movements of the right wing of the German Armies was now more easily appreciated, the circumstances in which they had to be carried out were very difficult. The complicated advance through Aix-la-Chapelle had to be begun before the ammunition and supply columns of the leading corps had finished detraining, and before the fighting troops of the corps following in the second line had been assembled, so that the separate corps could not be given sufficient time to complete their concentration and close up. Both the Reserve Corps had, immediately after a railway journey lasting some days, been obliged to make a most exhausting march in the hottest weather.

The march-formation of the First Army consisted of a deep column of two corps on each of the three roads, passing close to one another through Aix-la-Chapelle, and which did not greatly diverge between there and the Meuse, north of Liège, or even for some way beyond the river. A General was appointed to look after each of these three roads, and to issue all the necessary routine orders for the march. Billeting and supply columns were hurriedly sent forward from the railway base, as the Army Commander had ordered that every man was to be fully rationed by the time the Meuse was reached. Howitzer batteries were put into position near Aix-la-Chapelle by order of the Army Commander, to guard against air attacks; and all the roads along the Dutch frontier on the right flank of the advance were blocked. The Army Commander also ordered that the roads of advance should be thoroughly inspected and fully repaired, and all bridges and other constructions guarded.

Whether considered collectively or in detail, these movements and the careful supply of such a mass of men by three roads all passing through such a comparatively small town form a most valuable mine of information for instruction and historical purposes.

In a life full of military activities the Army Commander never witnessed such a stirring spectacle as that march of enthusiastic and endless columns through the historic streets of Aix-la-Chapelle.

To enable the further deployment of the Army to be carried out as rapidly as possible, the Army Commander ordered that the Train, or the supply sections of it, should march immediately in rear of each division; a two days' supply of food should be carried in rear of the second division, and the remainder of the first echelon of the ammunition columns and Train should move at the end of each column. The second echelon of transport of each pair of corps was to be massed and to march at a certain distance behind the rear corps. In order to ease the difficulties of their advance, Reserve Corps, as already mentioned, were to be detrained as near the front as possible, and were themselves to fix the length of their marches. In addition to much other preliminary work, Generalleutnant Telle, in his capacity as chief of the pioneers of the First Army, undertook the reconnaissance of the Meuse and its canals, and the necessary arrangements for bringing up bridging material, constructing bridges, and preparing river crossings, and for securing the safety of the latter. The initial plans for the attack on Antwerp were also considered at Grevenbroich on the basis of the appreciations available.

On the morning of the 12th August, while the reconnaissances and the preliminary troop-movements were being rapidly carried out, the news arrived of the fall of Fort Evegnée, which lies south-east of Fort Barchon. The bombardment of Forts Fléron and Chaudfontaine, south of those just mentioned, and on the eastern side of Liège, was to begin that evening. The line of forts on the north-east front was, however, already broken into, thus giving room for the First Army to move forward. On the following day at 9 a.m. the advance took place, without interruption, towards the line Visé–Herstal on the Meuse. The main bodies of the advanced guards of the corps reached their destinations as follows: II Corps Sippenaeken, IV Corps Hombourg, and III Corps Lontzen. The corps on the right-hand road were to continue their march by Sinnich–St. Martin–Fouron le Comte, on Lixhe and Visé; the centre corps were to march by Chevemont–Hagelstein–Neufchâteau on Argenteau; those on the left-hand road by Crosenberg–Henrichapelle–Clermont–Battice–Barchon on Herstal. The last-named places on each of the three roads were in the Meuse valley. Army Headquarters moved from Grevenbroich to Aix-la-Chapelle, the Army Commander being hospitably received by Von Sandt, the President of the Board of Government. Von Sandt held a similar position at Brussels after its occupation, and afterwards at Warsaw, where he succumbed to the strain of his duties. He was a great loss.

The IX Corps evacuated in good time the country south of the road on which the III Corps was marching, and direct communication between these two corps was established. The bridges over the Meuse at Visé and Argenteau were reported to have been destroyed, though that at Herstal was capable of limited use; at Lixhe, north of Visé, a temporary bridge had in the meantime been constructed, and at Visé one was in course of construction.

At 5.25 p.m. Second Army Headquarters reported the capture of Fort Pontisse. Situated in a commanding position on the left bank of the Meuse, it had till now barred the section of the river between Liège and the Dutch frontier which had to be crossed by the First Army. The passage of the river by large bodies of troops was now rendered feasible, and valuable time was thus gained for the deployment of the First Army and the development of the plan of campaign in the west. General von Emmich, with Generalmajor Ludendorff as Brigade-Commander, had broken the chain of forts on the north-eastern front of the fortress, in spite of their modern construction. Forts Liers and Lantin, west of Pontisse, were still temporarily a disturbing factor in the calculations of the Army Commander.

Information concerning the Belgian Army gave the impression that three or four divisions were in the area Louvain–Wavre, with advanced troops on the front Diest–Tirlemont; besides these, a division had been located at Antwerp and another at Namur. French troop trains appeared to be on their way to Brussels and to the front Namur–Dinant, whilst the British were said to be disembarking in small numbers at Ostend, and with larger forces at Dunkirk and Calais.[2] Cavalry reported a strong concentration of the enemy's cavalry east of Brussels.

At the request of the First Army Commander, the Second Army Commander ordered the 9th Cavalry Division, which for some time had been on the right bank of the Meuse south-west of Liège, to rejoin the command of General von der Marwitz. His divisions were suffering from want of oats and shortage of ammunition: they were helped out of their difficulties by a motor-transport column, rapidly organized and taken forward by Captain von Lekow, a highly efficient member of the Army Commander's staff.

Major Gedel, a French officer, in his book published in January, 1916, 'La Campagne, 1914: La Bataille de la Marne,' gives the strength of the Belgian Army at the outbreak of war as 117,000 men, 93,000 rifles, 6,000 sabres, 324 guns, and 102 machine guns. On the 3rd August this army of six infantry and one cavalry division was apparently disposed as follows: 1st Division on the march from Ghent to Thienen (Tirlemont); 2nd on the march from Antwerp to Louvain; 5th on the march from Mons to Perwez; 6th on the march from Brussels to Wavre; 4th, garrison of Namur; 3rd, garrison of Liège. The cavalry division was on its way to Varenne, though Gedel does not mention whence it had come.

According to information received and the general opinion at Army Headquarters, it was not thought likely that the main portion of the Belgian Army would operate as a combined force. If this proved to be the case, it was a most favourable circumstance for the success of the First Army in the difficult task of emerging from the defile Aix-la-Chapelle–Visé–Herstal in columns thirty to forty-five miles long. Events would have shaped very differently had the Belgian Army succeeded in offering, or even had it been intended to offer, an energetic resistance to the advance of the First and Second Armies with its whole force, basing its operations on Liège, Huy, and Namur, and preventing the bursting open of the line of forts; a most serious loss of time would thereby have been imposed upon the German flank armies. And in the eventful course of a struggle of nations, a saving of time means, besides much else, a saving of

---

2. No British troops landed at these ports until some weeks after the period in question. The B.E.F. disembarked mainly at Le Havre.

the precious lives of gallant and devoted warriors. Every leader should be alive to this fundamental principle, daily, hourly, and, above all, in times of crises. And this is true, first and foremost, of the Army Commander; for his example will inspire the mental attitude of all his subordinates.

This guiding principle is the vital factor in higher leading where a rapid success is in view, and its working may be traced both in the series of battles that were immediately ahead of us, and in the desperate struggle on the Marne. The latter contest is a signal illustration of this governing law of open warfare, and will supply dramatic and overwhelming proofs of its truth, both on our side and on the enemy's – *Lege artis praeceptiva*.

On the 14th August, the leading corps of the First Army – namely, the II, IV, and III Corps – reached the Meuse, and the two Reserve Corps, marching as a second line, began to pass the Belgian frontier west of Aix-la-Chapelle. On the 15th, the II Corps arrived at Bilsen, twelve miles west of Maestricht, the IV Corps at Membrüggen, while the III reached Nederheim, near Tongres, and so were close to the crossings of the Demer. The Army was thus clear of the narrow and troublesome defile between Liège and the Dutch frontier. In agreement with the Supreme Command, the First Army was given time to close up as soon as it was in possession of the line of the Demer.

After the fall of Forts Liers and Lantin, the forts that still held out on the south-west and southern front of Liège were quickly taken with the help of the 42 cm. howitzers. The IX Corps was placed under the orders of the First Army, and the brigades of the III and IV Corps, which had been employed against Liège, rejoined their corps on the 16th. On the 14th, the VII Corps, on the right flank of the Second Army, reached Lantin, close to the fort of that name on the north-western front of line of forts, which was now quite broken through. The Belgians were some way from the line of the Meuse, behind the Gette, on the front Diest–Tirlemont and at Wavre, with detachments also at Louvain farther west. The last forts on the southern circumference of Liège fell during the day, and the fortress at Huy was captured. It appeared that the French I and II Corps in the Namur section of the Meuse were still sending reinforcements from the south-west on to their left flank, on the right of the Belgians. It was hoped that a rapid advance of the right wing of the German Armies would defeat any hostile plans in that district, or at least seriously affect them.

In view of this situation, the First Army continued its advance on the 17th August, whilst the Second Army halted. The advanced guard of the II Corps reached Kermpt, on the Hasselt–Diest railway; that of the IV Corps, Stevort; that of the III Corps, Gorssum, north-west of St. Trond; that of the IX Corps, Brusthem, south-east of St. Trond; that of the III Reserve Corps, Visé; and that of the IV Reserve Corps, St André, the two last-named being on the east of the defile leading westwards. Army Headquarters was moved from Aix-la-Chapelle to Glons, passing through Liège, where a conference was held between the commanders of the German right wing, consisting of the First and Second Armies, and of the Chiefs of the Army Staffs.

At 4.30 p.m. the following order arrived from the Supreme Command: 'The First and Second Armies and the II Cavalry Corps (Marwitz) will be under the orders of the commander of the Second Army during the advance north of the Meuse. This advance will begin on the 18th August. It is most important that the enemy's forces reported to be in position between Diest–Tirlemont–Wavre should be shouldered away from Antwerp. It is intended to initiate further operations of both armies from the line Brussels–Namur, and measures must be taken to secure their flank against Antwerp.'

No reasons were given for thus unexpectedly placing the flank armies under one commander. The commander of the First Army considered that the measure would limit his powers of command, and that it might apparently have been avoided if timely directions had been sent to both armies, and if Marwitz's Cavalry Corps had been placed at the disposal of the First Army. It could have been foreseen that the Second Army, supported as it was on both flanks, would probably be confronted more especially with tactical problems, whereas the First Army would be faced by a situation pre-eminently strategical in its aspects. It seemed possible that, owing to the pressure of the situation on the First Army, divergent opinions might crop up which would make matters still more difficult for it. However, the second sentence of the Supreme Command order coincided with the views of the First Army Commander and his Chief of the Staff.

On the evening of the 17th August, the four corps of the first line arrived within striking distance of the Belgian Army on the Gette.

The Gette, a tributary of the Demer, flows in a winding course through wide meadows; in many places the bottom is soft, so that it can only be crossed at the bridges, or where improvised ones have been made. Dykes and wire fences hinder free movement. The First Army was concerned with the lower reach of the stream, where it forms a salient towards the east, thus lending itself to a concentric attack from that direction through the villages of Haelen, Geet Betz, Budingen, and Tirlemont. The breadth and depth of the obstacles vary, owing to side branches. The ground on the western bank overlooks the eastern bank, especially near Diest and Haelen, also west of Budingen and north of Tirlemont.

The Army Order for the 18th August, issued from Army Headquarters at Glons, at 11.15 p.m. on the 17th, was as follows:

'1. The enemy is in position on the line Diest–Tirlemont–Wavre, with strong forces in rear, probably near Louvain.

'2. The Army will attack tomorrow and envelop the enemy's left wing, driving him away from Antwerp. The II Corps will send one division by Beeringen–Pael–Veerle, and the other by Kermpt–Lummen–Diest round the enemy's flank. The IV Corps will march by Herck la Ville and Rummen towards Haegen and Geet Betz; it will leave three battalions, a section of cavalry, and three batteries of artillery at Stevoort, at the disposal of the Army Commander, by 8.30 a.m. The III Corps will move by Nieuwerkerken and Gorssum on Budingen and Neerlinter. The IX Corps will march from about St. Trond on Oplinter and Tirlemont, and will keep a strong reserve on its left flank to act against a possible enemy advance from the area south-west of Tirlemont.

'3. The 2nd Cavalry Division will be at the disposal of the Army Commander. It will move past Veerle, in order to cut off the retreat of the enemy.

'4. The corps will cross the line Pael–Lummen–St. Trond at 8 a.m.

'5. With the exception of the first line transport, the train and ammunition and supply columns will not go beyond the line Hasselt–Looz.

'6. Air reconnaissances will be carried out by the II Corps to the north of Demer towards Antwerp, by the IV Corps towards Aerschot and Malines, by the III Corps in the Louvain district, and by the IX Corps in the area Tirlemont–Wavre.

'7. The III Reserve Corps will march by Bilsen on Beverst: Corps Headquarters at Bilsen.

'8. The IV Reserve Corps will march by Argenteau on Tongres: Corps Headquarters at Tongres.

'9. Army Headquarters will be at Stevoort at 8.30 a.m., by which time the corps are to be in telephonic communication with it.

'10. The Second Army is to reach Vamont with its right wing, the VII Corps, by midday tomorrow. The First Army is to be under the orders of the Second Army Commander.

'All times will be given according to German standard time.

'(*Signed*) v. Kluck.'

These orders seemed a suitable introduction to the objects of the offensive. The co-operation of French with Belgian troops would be prevented, or was at least hindered, although the Second Army had had to halt during the 17th. From midday on the 18th its VII Corps, with strong reserves of the IX Corps, would cover the left flank of the First Army. A further attack on a broad front, probably with superior numbers, to gain ground towards Louvain–Brussels was provided for; the Belgian Army would be brought to battle in a difficult low-lying country, and forced away from Antwerp, as well as cut off from its communications with that fortress. By placing a strong reserve in echelon behind the left flank, precautions had been taken to prevent any interference with the attack of the IX Corps and also of the III Corps. The mass of Marwitz's Cavalry Corps was under the sole orders of the Second Army Commander, and employed in operations elsewhere, with objectives a long way westwards. On the 17th, all the fighting troops of the Reserve Corps of the First Army were clear of the Meuse defiles. The First Army was organized in two groups, four corps in front and two in reserve. Strong forces from the latter would shortly have to wheel up towards the south front of Antwerp. Such was the general situation at the moment.

The enemy withdrew in places before contact with the attacking troops, though in front of the II Corps at Diest and of the IX Corps at Tirlemont considerable resistance was first offered. The retirement of the enemy's centre was carried out in good time, and the resistance on the flanks showed good leadership and answered the enemy's purpose. The Belgian Army retired to an apparently prepared position on the line Rillaer–Winghe St. Georges–high ground west of Tirlemont.

By the evening of the 18th the pursuing troops of the First Army had reached the line Hersselt–Montaigu–Winghe St. Georges–Glabbeek Suerbempde–Tirlemont. No French troops had been observed with the Belgians. The cautious withdrawal of the Belgian Army led to the conclusion that, at the moment, it felt that in Flanders the Germans had superior numbers, and therefore preferred to take advantage of the Brialmont defences round Antwerp, rather than accept an unequal combat in the field. A further rapid advance of the First Army towards Brussels would no doubt clear up the situation, the Second Army following, echeloned on the left of the First Army.

From the moment the Belgian frontier was crossed the advance of the Army had suffered by treacherous acts on the part of the population, apparently instigated thereto by the local authorities. Firing from behind hedges was an act of daily occurrence, and horrible murders of officers and men, in which Belgian soldiers in civilian clothing participated, were frequent. International law was completely disregarded. Proclamations warning and threatening the population had no effect, so that a severe and inexorable system of reprisals had to be applied by the commanders on the spot, to put an end to this state of things. Punishments under martial law, the shooting of individuals, and the burning of houses, became numerous along and behind the front, but were slow in remedying the evil. It was advisable, whether in or out of quarters, to have a rifle handy, even for the divisional and other staffs some way behind the front. Each quarter occupied by the Army Commander had to be guarded by a battalion of infantry, with machine guns and single field guns, ready for action. These evil practices on the part of the population ate into the very vitals of the Army until the southern frontier of Belgium was reached. The communications and country in rear of the Army and its reserves had to be protected against these base, sometimes bestial, attacks in a most thorough manner, so as to prevent their repetition against troops following later.

Meanwhile the Lines of Communication Headquarters were moved forward to Aix-la-Chapelle, and on the 19th that area was extended up to the Meuse. They rendered the most valuable services to the First Army during the advance to the Seine and during the battle on the Ourcq, as well as in the trench warfare that followed. On the 19th, a new bridge for heavy traffic was completed at Visé, and preparations were made to move the Lines of Communication Headquarters to Tongres and then to

St. Trond. After making bridgeheads, the 10th *Landwehr* Brigade occupied all the river-crossings between Visé and Herstal, thereby relieving the detachments of the first line troops who had previously guarded them. The 11th *Landwehr* Brigade was brought up to Tongres, and the 27th to Aix-la-Chapelle. From the zone of operations of the Army back to the Meuse the two Reserve Corps guarded the lines of communication by means of flying columns; in the home territory this duty was carried out by *Landsturm* troops, who also provided the frontier guards. On the 17th, the second echelons of the leading corps were brought up, or commenced coming up, in front of the Reserve Corps in their corps areas.

At 10 p.m. on the 18th August the following Army Order and summary of the situation was issued from the Army Headquarters at Stevoort:

'1. The First Army drove back the enemy today at Diest and Tirlemont.

'2. French forces are reported to be advancing from Charleroi towards Gembloux.

'3. Tomorrow the First Army will continue its advance, pushing back the enemy in front of it, and its advanced guards will reach the line Campenhut–Bossut (north-east of Wavre). It will cross the line Aerschot–Meldert (south-west of Tirlemont) at 10 a.m. The II Corps will march by Aerschot–Wesemael–Wegegabel (south of Werchter)–Thieldonck–Vierstratten; it will protect its right flank, especially its trains and columns, against Antwerp; the fortress guns cover the northern roads west of Aerschot. The IV Corps will move by Winghe St. Georges–Linden–north side of Louvain–Velthem. The III Corps will march by Bautersem–south side of Louvain–Berthem. The IX Corps will march by Meldert–Tourinnes–Mille–Neerysche–Loonbeck. [Limits of corps areas were also given.]

'4. The 2nd Cavalry Division will be in position in front of the right wing early in the morning, and will advance through Aerschot towards Brussels, reconnoitring towards Antwerp and westwards on both sides of Brussels.

'5. The III Reserve Corps, moving through Hasselt, will reach Lummen with its advanced guard: Corps Headquarters at Hasselt. The IV Reserve Corps, marching by St. Trond, will reach Dormael with its advanced guard: Corps Headquarters at St. Trond. The line Kermpt–St. Trond is not to be passed before 2 p.m., by which time the transport of the front corps will have left that line.

'6. The right wing of the Second Army will reach Grez Doiceau tomorrow.

'7. Army Headquarters will be at Winghe St. Georges, and corps will be in telephonic communication with it by 10.30 a.m.

'8. Air reconnaissances will be carried out by the II Corps towards Antwerp; by the IV Corps in a westerly direction past the north of Brussels; by the III Corps in a westerly direction south of Brussels; and by the IX Corps in a south-westerly direction over Wavre.

'(*Signed*) v. Kluck.'

On the 19th, the corps reached their destinations as ordered, only meeting slight opposition in places. The enemy's forces, consisting of the 1st, 2nd, and 3rd Infantry Divisions, retired, as their situation demanded, in a westerly and north-westerly direction. At Werchter the 2nd Cavalry Division engaged the Belgian 5th and 6th Infantry Regiments, which apparently belonged to the Antwerp garrison: on the arrival of the II Corps in the fight the 2nd Cavalry Division went into billets at Aerschot, while the infantry advanced guards of the II Corps pushed on to Haecht–Ligseveld. Army Headquarters moved forward to Louvain. Proclamations by the Belgian Government inciting the civil population to fire on the enemy were found in this town, as well as corpses of women with rifles in their hands, killed during the fighting.

After the presence of the Belgian 1st, 2nd, and 3rd Infantry Divisions in front of the First Army had been established, confirmatory information arrived of the advance of French forces, their right flank moving from Charleroi towards Gembloux; further, a report came in that the French 5th Cavalry Division had retired from near Pervez, with heavy loss, under the fire of Marwitz's 4th and 9th Cavalry Divisions. The position of the First Army seemed to be in accord with the needs of the general situation. Serious interference with the advance from Antwerp could henceforward scarcely be feared. Brussels was to be occupied on the 20th, whilst the III Reserve Corps was to push on through Aerschot, observing Antwerp, and the IV Reserve Corps through Tirlemont.

An order from the Second Army Commander for the 20th demanded 'the line Ninove–Gembloux to be reached, and the Brussels–Gembloux railway to be crossed by 9 a.m.' From the very position of the corps, the nearer of these two objectives could not be reached by the time ordered, nor the farther one within the course of a day. This order could not therefore be complied with, in view both of the necessity for carefully maintaining the strength of every man and horse for the heavy fighting to come, and of the great demands that had already been made on their powers. The troops would therefore have to be allowed considerably more time in which to reach the lines ordered.

After offering only slight opposition the Belgian divisions retired across the Dyle on the 19th August, a move which, combined with information gathered from intercepted letters, seemed to indicate the arrival of British troops on the Belgian left flank.

In the Army Order issued from Louvain at 8 a.m. on the 20th August, the corps were informed that the First and Second Armies would continue the advance that day towards the line Ninove–Gembloux and that the VII Corps, on the right wing of the Second Army, would march by Arthennes–Okembourg–northern part of Wavre–Rosières–Ohain. The march orders for the First Army were:

'II Corps by Vilvorde and Koningsloo, guarding its flank against Antwerp and Ganshoren (north-west of Brussels); IV Corps by Kortenberg–centre of Brussels–Anderlecht (west of the capital); III Corps by Tervueren–Boitsfort–Droogebosch (south of Brussels); IX Corps by Overysche Hoeylaert–La Hulze–Waterloo. The II and IV Corps will arrive on a level with Brussels by noon; the III Corps will cross the Brussels–Gembloux railway at 10.30 a.m., and the IX Corps will cross it at 9.30 a.m. The II Corps will send out patrols towards the line Termonde–Alost, the IV Corps towards Ninove, the III Corps towards Enghien, and the IX Corps through Ittres and Braine le Comte. Air reconnaissances will be carried out by the II Corps over the railways and roads in the area Vilvorde (north-east of Brussels)–Termonde–Alost–Ninove–Brussels and Louvain–Antwerp; by the III Corps in the area Brussels–Ninove–Renaix–Mons–Brussels; by the IX Corps in the area Louvain–Mons–Charleroi–Wavre.

'The 2nd Cavalry Division, working in concert with the II Corps, will patrol all the practicable roads immediately in front of the right wing of the First Army, and, advancing between Brussels and Antwerp, will discover the line of advance of the British troops. This duty is of urgent importance. The III Reserve Corps will march by Blankelaer and Diest to Betecom, preparatory to covering the flank of the Army towards Antwerp. The IV Reserve Corps will march by Tirlemont, and reach Roosbeek with its advanced guard. The ammunition columns and train of the leading corps must be forward of a line Aerschot–Tirlemont by noon.'

At the moment of issuing this order a report came in from the II Corps that, owing to the occupation of Wespelaer by the enemy, the corps had only reached the line Lipseveld–Wackerzeel on the previous day, the 19th, and that, in view of the fighting and the marches of the last few days, in addition to the difficulties of the supply services, the corps could only march as far as Vilvorde in the current day, the 20th. A request was also made that a shorter march might be ordered for the corps on the 21st, as the rear division had to push up to the head of the column to relieve the leading division.

The 2nd Cavalry Division, advancing between Antwerp and Brussels, arrived, during the day, at Wolwerthem, where its presence had been anxiously awaited by the Army Commander. The VII Corps of the Second Army, marching in close touch with the IX Corps of the First Army, reached west of Ohain. The left wing of the Second Army began the attack on Namur.

On the 20th August the disposition of the First Army was therefore as follows: 2nd Cavalry Division about Wolwerthem; II Corps advanced guard at Vilvorde; III Reserve Corps advanced guard west of Aerschot in deep march formation opposite the south front of the Antwerp forts, without being molested or noticed by the garrison; IV, III, and IX Corps west and south of Brussels, facing south-west towards Enghien, the IX Corps being in touch with the VII Corps of the Second Army; IV Reserve Corps about Tirlemont as general reserve of the Army, so placed that it could reach any part of the Army front to north, west, or south in one or two marches. The maps in the Appendix to this book will make these dispositions easier to follow, and give the situation as it appeared at the time.

Of the initial movements of the Army up to the end of the first great stride from Aix-la-Chapelle to Brussels, the Memorandum says as follows:

'By the occupation of Brussels the first objective of the Army has been obtained. The unexpected swiftness and smoothness of the advance, while it subjected both combatant and non-combatant troops to the utmost conceivable strain, completely surprised the Belgian Army and frustrated all its hopes of support from the forces of England and France. The combined operations by Belgian, British, and perhaps French troops, which had been so carefully planned beforehand, have failed, and the rapid occupation of Belgium has thereby been made possible. In spite, however, of isolated cases of obstinate resistance, the Belgians have always managed to escape our grasp, so that their Army has not been decisively beaten nor forced away from Antwerp. It has, nevertheless, been so severely handled that a comparatively small force will be able to contain it in Antwerp and prevent it from taking part in the decisive fighting. The advance of the Army was very greatly complicated, though not actually delayed, by the resistance of the population, encouraged by the local authorities and the Press. Assisted by soldiers in plain clothes, it waged an extremely aggressive guerrilla warfare, making the roads unsafe behind the front, and particularly interfering with our telephone cables.'

Had the German Army been mobilized and deployed three days earlier, a more sweeping and decisive result would probably have been gained. At the outbreak of war time is always of the greatest importance, and in certain situations it is vital. Remember Napoleon's '*Vitesse, vitesse.*'[3]

According to the first despatch of Sir John French, commanding the British Expeditionary Force, to the Secretary of State for War, dated 7th September, 1914, it appears that the plan of landing the British Army on the Belgian coast was abandoned at the outset, and instead the more secure landing-places, Dunkirk, Calais, and Boulogne[4] were selected, in agreement with the French Government. After a consultation between Field-Marshal French and General Joffre it was agreed that the British should then move up to a deployment zone Condé–Mons–Maubeuge, and, as will be seen later, by the 22nd August the British Army was ready to give battle, or at least was completing its deployment, in this area. The desire of the Army Commander to attack and disperse the British and Belgian divisions before leaving Flanders was not to be fulfilled.

---

3. What Napoleon wrote to Marshal Massena on 18th April, 1809, was: '*Activité, activité, vitesse! Je me recommande à vous.*' It was a postscript, in Napoleon's own handwriting, to the letter given in *Correspondance* 15087.
4. There is no mention of these ports in Sir John French's Despatch, and the two first-named ports were not used. As will be seen, Von Kluck was obsessed with the idea that the B.E.F. had landed at the places he names here, and that its communications ran east and west.

Chapter Two

Brussels–Somme

The Battles with the British Expeditionary Force –
The Pursuit – General d'Amade's Army

On the 20th August, as was mentioned in the previous chapter, the Army Commander was still counting on the possible co-operation of British troops with the Belgian Army. In these circumstances, the following dispositions of the First Army at that date appeared to meet the situation: IV Corps at Brussels; II Corps at Vilvorde and east of Malines, opposite the southern front of the Antwerp defences, with the 2nd Cavalry Division at Wolwerthem in front of the above two corps; the III Reserve Corps west and east of Aerschot and south-east of Antwerp; the IV Reserve Corps north-west and east of Tirlemont; the III Corps south of Brussels. The III, IV, and II Corps were thus ready to give battle at any moment against the front Wolwerthem–Termonde and towards the line Alost–Ninove; or, on the other hand, the IV, III, and IX could turn and fight southwards with their right flank covered by the II and III Reserve Corps as well as by the cavalry. The IV Reserve Corps in one or two marches could be employed, according to circumstances, either on the front Malines–Wolwerthem, or beyond the line Brussels–Wavre. The IX Corps about Waterloo could now be also regarded as a general reserve for operations to the north or west; or it might be treated as the pivot for a wheeling movement to the south-west.

The following are extracts from the Army Order of the 20th August, issued at 8 p.m.:

'The IV Corps entered Brussels today, without opposition. A great part of the Belgian Army has apparently retired on Antwerp: one infantry division is reported at Termonde. It is believed that the disembarkation of the British Expeditionary Force was completed in French harbours on the 18th August; the direction of its advance is unknown. The Second Army has begun the attack on Namur with its left wing, and is moving to meet the French force reported to be advancing on Gembloux; the VII Corps, on the right wing, is moving south of Mont St. Jean along the main road to Nivelles. The cavalry of the Second Army has inflicted a decisive defeat on a French cavalry division.'

As the Belgian Army had neither been dispersed nor forced away from Antwerp in spite of the rapid advance of the First Army, it now became of the utmost importance for the latter to protect the right flank of the German armies, not only against Antwerp, but also against the coast and the coastal provinces of Northern France. In order to be in a position to undertake this new and far-reaching duty, the First Army made a short advance on the 21st, with its right flank echeloned back and covering Antwerp. The II Corps reached Ganshoren with its leading troops, taking up a covering position, and sending out patrols west of the Dyle Canal between Louvain and Malines; the IV Corps entered Castre with its advanced guard; the III Corps arrived at Hal, and the IX Corps at Braine le Château, both with their leading troops; the duties of the 2nd Cavalry Division kept it near Wolwerthem; the III Reserve Corps was to be south of Aerschot and south of the Demer on the 22nd, ready to protect the flank of the Army against Antwerp east of the Dyle Canal between Louvain–Malines, and, if necessary, to be able to continue its advance in a westerly direction (the bend in the road at Haecht was believed to be under fire from the guns of the Antwerp forts). The IV Reserve Corps occupied Louvain with its advanced troops. The interval between the leading and rear divisions of both the Reserve Corps was to depend on the length of their day's march. The First Army was thus in such a position that the great majority of the troops could have a much-needed rest.

The Order also directed, as was now feasible, the second line transport of the II Corps to pass through the III Reserve Corps and join up with the first line transport of its corps, and for that of the IV Corps to move through Brussels or its southern suburbs, passing Louvain in good time, and avoiding the line of march of the III Corps. Special orders were given for guarding the corps ammunition depots against the population, also for protecting the bridge near the Gette at Haelen by the III Reserve Corps, and for the rapid restoration of the railway bridge west of St. Trond, with the help of the Lines of Communication troops, so that it might carry loaded motor lorries. Army Headquarters remained at Louvain.

The report that arrived on the 21st that the country as far as the line Ghent–Audenarde–Tournai was clear of the enemy was important. On this the Army Commander had to make up his mind as to the direction in which the advance was to be continued. According to the original instructions, the duties of the First Army, besides that of covering Antwerp and guarding its own communications, were, as has been repeatedly mentioned, the protection of the right flank of the German Armies against the Belgian Army and the British force which was supposed to be about to arrive, with or without French troops. An advance of British troops through the Lille district would now have to be taken into account, and it therefore seemed necessary to move the First Army more in a south-westerly direction, with its left flank passing west of Maubeuge, and keeping touch with the VII Corps of the Second Army. Whatever the direction of the enemy's advance, the First Army would then be in a position to turn south, west, or north-west to attack him. Also, more space for manoeuvre would be gained on the right – *i.e.,* to the westwards towards Tournai and Douai – which would prevent the First and Second Armies from interfering with each other's movements in the case of a further advance and a wheel southwards.

The Commander of the Second Army regarded the situation from a different point of view, and on the 21st August issued the following Army Order: 'The Second Army will advance on the 22nd to the line Binche–Jemeppe, and, by crossing the Sambre on the 23rd, enable the Third Army to cross the Meuse. The First Army, whilst observing Antwerp and holding Brussels, will so conform to this movement that, if needed, it will be able to operate west of Maubeuge in support of the Second Army after it has invested the north and north-east fronts of that fortress.' In reply to a protest by the First Army Commander, these instructions were upheld with the argument 'that otherwise the First Army might get too far away and not be able to support the Second Army at the right moment.' The Commander of the Second Army did not take into account the possible speedy appearance of British troops; this was probably due to the following communication issued by the Supreme Command on the 20th August, and received on the evening of the 21st, which ran: 'A landing of British troops at Boulogne and their advance from about Lille must be reckoned with. It is believed that a disembarkation of British troops on a big scale has not yet taken place.'

A more accurate appreciation of the situation was arrived at by First Army Headquarters at Louvain, as the future was to show. The British Army, as we now know according to the above-mentioned dispatch of Sir John French, was assembled on the Mons–Condé Canal, and near Binche on the 21st/22nd August.[1] The Commander of the Second Army urged that the First Army should keep close in to the Second, whereas it really needed a greater freedom of manoeuvre in order to carry out its allotted task, which was still primarily of a strategic nature, and intended to open the way to tactical successes. The decision of the Second Army Commander had its influence on the course of the operations against the British, and for days embarrassed the plans of the First Army Commander and his Chief of the Staff.

At noon on the 21st August a report arrived at Louvain by wireless that the 2nd, 4th, and 9th Cavalry Divisions were assembled under General von der Marwitz near Ath, and were under the orders of the Second Army Commander. Thus, regrettably, the First Army was not to have any large body of cavalry at its disposal, a serious deprivation in view of the need for rapid operations during the wheeling movement of the Army.

The Army Order of the 21st, issued from Louvain at 9.30 p.m., informed the corps that air reconnaissances reported Termonde evacuated by the enemy and the country free in the direction Ghent–Ostende, as was also the area Audenarde–Ath–Tournai. South of the Sambre enemy forces were advancing in a northerly direction between Namur and Maubeuge, and the Second Army was to advance on the 22nd August with its right wing, the VII Corps, moving from Nivelles to Binche. Marwitz's Cavalry Corps was to march with its 2nd Division by Nederbrakel, half-way between Grammont and Audenarde, its 4th Division by Enghien, and its 9th Division by Soignies.

The First Army was also to wheel to the left in support of the Second Army. The advanced guards of its leading corps were given destinations as follows: II Corps to Ninove, Corps Headquarters at Dilbeck; IV Corps, Ollignies–Silly, Corps Headquarters at Enghien; III Corps, Thoricourt–Chaussée Notre Dame Louvignies, Corps Headquarters at Rebecq Rognon;

---

1. The author antedates the assembly there by a day. There was only a cavalry brigade at Binche.

IX Corps, Langrenée–Mignault, Corps Headquarters at Braine le Comte. Army Headquarters were to be at Louvain till midday, when they would move through Brussels to Hal. The Army Commander would then be nearer the front of the Army and in close touch with the Corps Headquarters.

The III Reserve Corps was to send a detachment of all arms early in the morning to the neighbourhood of Campenhout, six miles south of Malines, to protect the ammunition and supply columns of the II Corps, which were to follow their corps on the 22nd. The III Reserve Corps was to advance at midday and occupy a position astride the reach of the Dyle Canal between Louvain and Malines, in order to guard the flank of the Army against Antwerp, Corps Headquarters at Thildonck. The IV Reserve Corps was to reach Brussels.

The order also directed long-distance reconnaissances to be made by the III Reserve Corps through Vilvorde to Opwyck, by the II Corps to the line Alost–Grootenberge–Lessines, and by the IV, III, and IX Corps to the line Ath–Mons–Givry, six miles north of the Maubeuge forts. Communication was to be maintained with the Cavalry Corps on the whole front of this wide reconnaissance zone. To the devoted and untiring activity of the flying section of the II Corps was allotted the area Audenarde–Courtrai–Lille; to that of the III Corps, the area Tournai–Lille–Douai; and to that of the IX Corps, the area Valenciennes–Maubeuge–Solesmes. Reports were to be sent in immediately to Louvain or Hal. The formation and direction of march of the Army were such that it could be employed according to its commander's own view of the situation. The Second Army intended to reach the line Binche–Mellet during the day.

The presence of British troops in front of the Second Army was established in the course of the 22nd August: a squadron of cavalry was reported at Casteau, north-east of Mons,[2] and a British aeroplane, which had come from Maubeuge on a reconnaissance flight, was shot down. The Mons–Condé Canal was found to be occupied between Mons and Ville sur Haine, though, on the other hand, the country west of it as far as the Schelde, as also Lille and the railways leading westwards, were reported free of the enemy. The presence of British troops in front of

---

2. This agrees with British accounts that contact first took place at Casteau.

the First Army was also certain, though it was not certain whether the mass of the British Army had yet arrived near Maubeuge. It seemed to the First Army Commander all the more important to aim at outflanking the British left wing by keeping the First Army well away to westward as a strong right wing.

When, on inquiring of the Supreme Command, it was understood that the First Army would remain for the time being under the orders of the Second Army Commander, a General Staff Officer was sent to the latter to represent the arguments against adopting the march direction ordered for the left wing of the First Army. The Second Army Commander gave as his reason for ordering the close co-operation of the First and Second Armies that the latter had all its leading troops already in action on the Sambre, with heavy fighting in places: also that the Third Army might find itself in a difficult situation when crossing the Meuse. It was then suggested that the left wing of the First Army might advance by Mons towards Bavai, but in vain! On the other hand, the idea of using the First Army to invest the north-east front of Maubeuge was abandoned, and instead it was directed to send a division to take up a position at Givry to support the VII Corps, as the Second Army was to attack on the 23rd with its right wing moving from Binche towards Solre.

General von der Marwitz assembled his three cavalry divisions in the area Renaix–Ath–Leuze, turning with the mass of his corps from a southerly to a north-westerly direction.

The proposal of the First Army Commander to keep his Army out on the western flank away from the Second Army was thus refused, and this at a time when the fateful crisis on the western wing of the German armies was approaching. Had the First Army been free and untrammelled, it would probably have been in a position to outflank and crush the British Army by coming in against it from the west, and, investing Maubeuge, to force it back on to the French Fifth Army, and then take them both in rear.

The increasing length of the communications demanded a careful organization in rear of the First Army. Oh the 22nd August the Supreme Command placed 20 battalions and 4 squadrons of *Landsturm* troops at its disposal, and on the same day they were handed over to the Commander of the Lines of Communication to be used between

Aix-la-Chapelle and the front. All the *Landwehr* troops thus freed from communication work were to be sent to reinforce the III Reserve Corps, to increase the force covering the rear of the Army, and on the 24th the 27th *Landwehr* Brigade was sent to Waenrode, south-west of Diest, for the same purpose. The detachments left behind by the fighting corps to guard the communications were to be relieved as quickly as possible, and sent forward to rejoin their units. To assist the work of supply, a light-railway system up to the corps was successfully opened for traffic on the 22nd August – that for the II Corps to Ninove and Vollezeel; for the IV Corps at first to Castre, later to Enghien; and for the III Corps to Hal. The IX Corps was ordered to restart navigation on the Brussels–Hal–Tubize Canal as rapidly as practicable. The Army Intendant was responsible for keeping the store depots in Brussels well supplied and maintaining supply reserves.

When Army Headquarters arrived at Hal, instructions were issued for masking Maubeuge, and for engaging the line of barrier forts between Lille and Maubeuge, as it could not possibly be foreseen that they would be evacuated without offering opposition.

As regards Maubeuge, it was intended to place a force of suitable strength outside the range of the outer forts, which could effectively deal with enemy attacks from advanced positions covered by the fortress artillery.

The line of barrier forts between Lille and Maubeuge included the obsolete forts of Maulde, Flines, and Curgies, and the old walled towns Valenciennes and Le Quesnoy. Maulde and Curgies were protected against assault, and so only the destruction of their guns and their investment was ordered. Flines was a fort of quite inferior quality.

It was assumed that the underground quarters of all these forts were proof against the fire of heavy howitzers. It was also possible that the River Schelde would be flooded between Flines and Condé. The breadth of the Schelde Canal in that district is about forty-eight feet.

Before entering on the account of the fighting of the First Army on the Mons–Condé Canal and west of Maubeuge, it seems advisable to consider for a moment the situation of the British Expeditionary Force according to the later despatches of Sir John French. By agreement with General Joffre, commanding-in-chief, it had completed its deployment by the 22nd, and, except for the III Corps, which had not yet arrived, was in position as follows: I Corps on a line Binche–Mons (exclusive);[3] II Corps between Mons and Condé, 5th Cavalry Brigade near Binche and the Cavalry Division behind the left flank of the II Corps. On the 22nd/23rd both these cavalry detachments sent reconnoitring squadrons towards Soignies. Nothing was definitely known of General Joffre's plan of campaign.

It was believed that one or two German corps with a cavalry division were opposed to the British force, and this seemed to be confirmed by the reports of air reconnaissances and patrols. On the afternoon of the 23rd General French received information that the Germans were attacking the 'Mons line'; the right wing from Mons to Bray was especially threatened, so that General Haig's I Corps had to bend back its right flank to the south of Bray,[4] and the 5th Cavalry Brigade had to withdraw southwards from Binche, which was immediately occupied by the Germans. At Mons itself the right wing of General Hamilton's 3rd Division was in position on the 23rd. It was threatened with being outflanked, and General French therefore ordered it to retire southwards before dark if the II Corps was seriously menaced. At 5 p.m. General Joffre sent the unexpected information that at least three German corps were advancing against the front of the British force, and one was threatening to outflank it from Tournai; and that the French Fifth Army and the two French Reserve Divisions were already in retreat, as the Germans had obtained possession of the Sambre crossings between Charleroi and Namur on the 22nd. According to his report, General French had already in view another position farther in rear, its right resting on Maubeuge and its left on Curgies, west of Jenlain, on the Maubeuge-Valenciennes road. On hearing of the French retreat, and realizing the German menace, he ordered the British Army to march back to this new position early on the 24th.

The foundation for the important battle of Mons was laid by the Army Order for the 23rd August, issued from Hal at 9.30 p.m. on the 22nd. It seems best to give it in full for the benefit of future historians:

---

3. The right of the I Corps was not at Binche (where there was a cavalry brigade), but six miles south-west of it, near Peissant.
4. Von Kluck's mistake as to the position of the right of the I Corps has been noticed in the previous footnote. Not being where he imagined it to be, it did not have to 'bend back' as he states.

'1. A squadron of British cavalry was encountered today at Casteau, north-east of Mons, and a British aeroplane coming from Maubeuge was shot down near Enghien. In front of the Second Army there appear today to be only three cavalry divisions and a weak force of infantry.[5]

'2. The Second Army has advanced today to the line Binche–Mettet, north-west of Dinant, and tomorrow it is to press forward east of Maubeuge, its right wing, the VII Corps, moving from Binche through Solre.

'3. The First Army will continue its advance tomorrow to the area north-west of Maubeuge, masking that fortress.

'4. The II Corps will reach La Hamaide, marching from Ninove through Grammont; the IV Corps will march to Basecles and Stambruges by Ath and Chièvres; the III Corps will reach St. Ghislain and Jemappes by Lens and Jurbise. The rising ground on the southern side of the canal is to be occupied. The IX Corps will cover the movement of the Army towards Maubeuge, and for this purpose will advance across the line Mons–Thieu towards the north and north-western front of Maubeuge, keeping its main force on its right flank. The line Ath–Roeulx will be crossed by the leading troops of the IV, III, and IX Corps by 8.30 a.m. [The lines of demarcation for the corps were then given.] Reconnaissances by corps cavalry will be carried out by the II Corps to the line Alost–Audenarde–Renaix–Leuze; by the IV Corps to the line Fort Maulde–Fort Flines–Valenciennes; and by the III Corps to the line Fort Curgies–Bavai. Air reconnaissances will be made by corps in their own reconnaissance area, the III Corps area belonging also to the IV Corps for this purpose. The Army Air Detachment will report on the area Douai–Cambrai–Le Cateau–Avesnes–Valenciennes. Corps Headquarters will send in their reports by 9.30 a.m.

'5. The IV Reserve Corps, marching by Hal, will reach Bierghes with its advanced guard; the III Reserve Corps will guard the right flank of the Army and its communications against the garrison of Antwerp. It will

---

5. As we know from narratives of German officers who took part in the action, the presence of the British on the Mons Canal came as a complete surprise. The German cavalry had reported the country clear for fifty miles (*vide* Captain Bloem's 'Vormarsch').

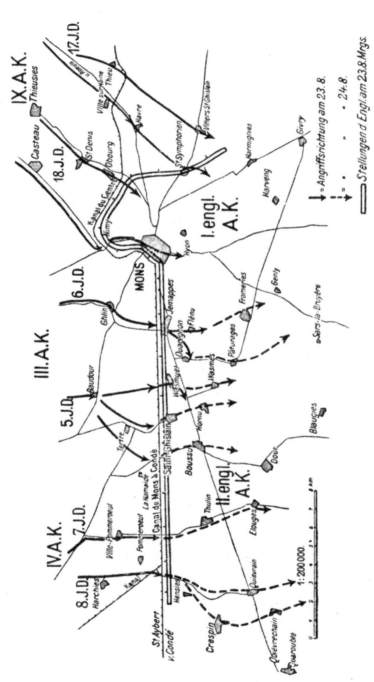

THE BATTLE OF MONS.

take up its position so that it can at the same time guard Brussels against possible raids. Special orders will be issued for the distribution of the *Landwehr* troops. On their arrival, the two battalions of the IV Reserve Corps now garrisoning Brussels will be relieved.

'6. During the further advance the operations against the Forts of Maulde and Flines will probably fall to the IV Corps, and those against Curgies to the III Corps. Reconnaissances of these places will be begun tomorrow if possible.

'7. An air reconnaissance by the II Corps today reported bivouac-fires, probably Belgian, about Alost-Grootenberge. The **II** Corps and IV Reserve Corps will clear up this matter and protect their march accordingly.

'8. Army Headquarters will be at Soignies, with which the Army Cable Detachment will have established communication by 11 a.m. The IX Corps will leave behind one battalion and two machine guns at Soignies from 8 a.m. onwards for guarding Army Headquarters.'

During this advance on the 22nd August, a report reached Army Headquarters that a detainment of troops had been in progress at Tournai since the previous day. It therefore seemed not unlikely that strong British forces were being sent forward through Lille.[6] The advanced guards of the corps were thereupon halted on the road Leuze–Mons–Binche to enable preparations to be made for the Army to wheel westwards. Thus, had the conjecture proved correct, the IV Corps was in a position to wheel at once from about Leuze towards Tournai, the right division of the III Corps could have moved by the afternoon by La Hamaide, followed later by the leading division of the II Corps, and on the 24th the rear division of the II Corps and the left division of the III Corps would have been up in line, followed during the evening by the leading troops of the IV Reserve Corps. It would have been the duty of the IX Corps to watch the canal position between St. Ghislain and Mons, to keep touch with the Second Army, and to guard the left flank and rear of the First Army; to assist it in doing this, it would have been

---

6. The troops in question were, of course, French – two battalions of the 176th Territorial Infantry Regiment (*vide* Mairesse's 'Tournai et La Retraite de Mons').

supported by as strong a detachment of the III Corps as the situation might demand.

In the earlier course of the campaign, the mobility of the different Army Corps had reached such a pitch as fully to warrant the confidence in it displayed by the higher command. Eventually, however, the presence of only one French infantry brigade was reported at Tournai, and that it was retiring on Lille. The Army therefore continued its advance.

On this day Marwitz's Cavalry Divisions watered their horses in the Schelde, west of Renaix. Oats lay in stooks in abundance in the fields.

The obstinate fighting for the crossings of the Mons–Condé Canal on the 23rd August, in which both sides suffered heavy losses, was the prelude, as General French reports, to a four days' uninterrupted battle.[7] The British Expeditionary Force fought excellently, while British prisoners extolled the Germans as attacking like devils. By the evening the IV Corps had advanced to immediately north of the line Hensies–Thulin; showing a praiseworthy grasp of the situation, they had pushed on beyond the appointed end of the day's march and crossed the canal between Condé and St. Ghislain. The III Corps fought with its right division about Tertre till well into the night, whilst its left division was able to cross the canal about Quaregnon–Jemappes and press forward to Flenu. The IX Corps had occupied the southern edge of Mons and taken St. Symphorien. Strong forces seemed to be in action on both sides all along the line. The Second Army reached Binche with its right wing, driving the enemy out of it.[8]

In their appreciation of the situation on the evening of the 23rd August, Army Headquarters at Hal considered that the following points demanded anxious attention:

Exploitation of today's successes by continuing to exert a uniformly strong pressure with the IV, III, and IX Corps.

Main objective of the operations to force the enemy into Maubeuge, each corps having a sharply defined zone of manoeuvre.

Avoidance of any bunching of troops west of Maubeuge.

Cutting and otherwise obstructing the communications of the British Army leading to the coast.

---

7. See Note 1, p. 58.

8. It was stated above (p. 30) that it was already occupied by the Germans

Keeping out of range of the outer forts of Maubeuge.

As a result of these and other considerations, the Army Order for the continuation of the attack on the 24th August, issued from Soignies at 8 p.m., was expressed in the following terms:

'The IX Corps will advance with its right wing direct from Mons, III Corps from the line St. Ghislain–Jemappes, and IV Corps on the front Crespin–Thulin. The attack is to be so directed that the enemy will be forced into Maubeuge and cut off from his line of retreat to the west. To this end the IX Corps will drive the enemy back to Maubeuge, and invest the north and north-west fronts of the fortress, with its right wing, if possible, about Bavai.

'The III Corps will advance with its left wing west of Bavai, and the IV Corps with its left wing on Wargnies Le Grand. A bunching of the Army near Maubeuge is to be avoided; the effective range of the fortress' artillery reaches to about a line Aulnoye–Bavai–Geeles, which must be watched. Fort Curgies is to be held in check by the IV Corps if there is a further advance.

'The II Corps will start at 2 a.m., and march first through Leuze to Condé. The Forts Maulde and Flines are to be silenced as soon as possible, so that the advance of the Army will not be interfered with. Colonel von Berendt of the Army Staff will supervise this operation.

'The IV Reserve Corps will start at 2 a.m. and march first by Ath to Lignes. At 6 a.m. it will send four more battalions to Brussels to reinforce the garrison. The Governor of Brussels, Major-General von Jarotski, will be under the orders of General von Beseler (III Reserve Corps). The IX Reserve Corps will shortly be sent up through Liège against Antwerp.

'General von der Marwitz has been ordered to advance on the right flank of the Army towards Denain, in order to bar the British line of retreat to the west.

'Constant communication between corps commanders and Army Headquarters at Soignies is absolutely necessary, and the corps commanders must keep in constant touch with their telephone stations, should they leave them, by motor-cars or other means. The II Corps and IV Reserve Corps will send to Soignies for orders at 10 a.m., and should there be no telephonic communication the IV, III, and IX Corps will send their representatives to Army Headquarters between 7 a.m. and 8 a.m.'

In spite of the usual constant uncertainty as to the enemy's situation in war, in the Army Commander's opinion there were two salient ideas by which the operations for the following days should be guided: 'The forcing of the British towards Maubeuge and south of it by means of the IV, III, and IX Corps (which has been already spoken of), and, in conformity with this, the rapid advance of the right wing of the Army, the II and IV Reserve Corps, in conjunction with the Cavalry Corps.' The manner in which the British Army was able to escape the destruction thus planned for it will shortly be seen.

The above-mentioned transport of the IX Reserve Corps by Aix-la-Chapelle towards Antwerp somewhat simplified the work of guarding the communications; until it arrived the IV Reserve Corps had unfortunately to go short of a complete infantry brigade used for this purpose.

In view of the uncertainty of the general situation, the Army Commander was anxiously wishing that Marwitz's Cavalry Corps should advance on Denain. On this day it had reached the Schelde about Berghem and Pottes, and had there received an order from the Second Army Commander to continue its advance on Courtrai – an operation which might well have been entrusted to a regiment of cavalry with some guns and machine guns. At the request of the First Army Commander, the Supreme Command placed General von der Marwitz at the disposal of the First Army. Although most valuable time had been thrown away and the fighting strength of the men and horses wasted by the protracted movement of his corps away to the north-west, it could, nevertheless, henceforth conform to the movements of the right wing of the First Army and should be able by an exceptional effort to reach the area north of Denain by the 24th.

The Second Army intended to continue its attack on the 24th, its right wing moving from Binche on Merbes-le-Château. At 12.7 a.m. (midnight) on the 24th the following order was received from the Second Army Headquarters, issued between 8 p.m. and 10.15 p.m. on the 23rd: 'The IX Corps will advance immediately west of Maubeuge to outflank the enemy's left wing; the III Corps will move in echelon behind the IX Corps and conform to its movements.' In addition to this, an order was sent direct to the IX Corps that the corps was to be alarmed and advance at once. In reply to this, a message was sent back that both the IX and III Corps were already in a battle position facing the enemy, the former on the front Mons–Villers–St. Ghislain, and that the advance ordered was therefore impracticable.

On the 24th August, after some heavy fighting, the leading troops of the IV, III, and IX Corps reached a line Onaing–Elouges–Dour–Genly–Harveng. The British force, estimated at from two to three divisions, was driven back[9] towards a line Curgies-Bavai. The II Corps took Condé after a short encounter with French territorial troops. The Forts Maulde and Flines, both being without artillery, were occupied without a fight, as was also the undefended Fort Curgies on the following day. The IV Reserve Corps reached Ligne, south-west of Ath. The main British force – or, according to a copy of orders found on the field, the whole Expeditionary Force – was believed to be between Valenciennes and Maubeuge. A weak detachment of troops from the Lille garrison was reported on the line Menin–Roubaix–Tournai. General von der Marwitz had dispersed a French infantry brigade near Tournai. According to a Second Army wireless message taken up by First Army Headquarters at Soignies, the Army had decisively beaten the enemy, in front of it, and was continuing its victorious advance.

After the severe opposition offered by the British Army in the two days' battle of Mons-St. Ghislain, a further and even stronger defence was to be expected on the line Valenciennes–Bavai–Maubeuge.

In the meantime, from the enemy's point of view the situation had developed as follows, according to Sir John French's despatch. At dawn on the 24th August, the 2nd British Division, supported by all the divisional artillery of the I Corps, began a 'demonstration' from Harmignies towards Binche, whilst the 1st Division at Peissant, south-west of Binche, prepared to make an advance: these movements were against the front of the German IX and VII Corps. Under the supposed protection of these demonstrations the British II Corps retired to a line Frameries–Dour–Quarouble, its right division, the 3rd, suffering heavy loss in the operation. The British II Corps then held the partially entrenched position on that line, whilst the I Corps retired during the morning to the line Maubeuge–Bavai. By midday General French arrived

---

9. Why drive them back if it were intended to envelop them? They retired, of course, by order.

at the conclusion that the Germans were directing their main attack against the British left wing, where the 5th Division was being heavily pressed, and where General Allenby's Cavalry Division, supporting it, had had very heavy casualties during an attack of the 9th Lancers and 18th Hussars against German infantry. The 19th Infantry Brigade, which had been previously guarding the communications and had been sent by rail to Valenciennes[10] on the 22nd/23rd August, covered the left flank of the British II Corps south of Quarouble, from the morning of the 24th onwards. Although greatly exhausted the corps effectively carried out its retreat with the assistance of the Cavalry Division, and by dusk had reached a position west of Bavai.

Thus the British Army was again ready to meet the German First Army in a second battle, with its I Corps between Maubeuge and Bavai, its II Corps about Bry and Jenlain – left flank supported by the 19th Infantry Brigade – and its Cavalry Division astride the Rhonelle stream.

Sir John French writes as follows in his despatch on the events of the next day, the 25th:

'The French were still retiring, and I had no support except such as was afforded by the Fortress of Maubeuge; and the determined attempts of the enemy to get round my left flank assured me that it was his intention to hem me against that place and surround me. I felt that not a moment must be lost in retiring to another position.

'I had every reason to believe that the enemy's forces were somewhat exhausted, and I knew that they had suffered heavy losses. I hoped, therefore, that his pursuit would not be too vigorous to prevent me effecting my object.

'The operation, however, was full of danger and difficulty, not only owing to the very superior force in my front, but also to the exhaustion of the troops.

'The retirement was recommenced in the early morning of the 25th to a position in the neighbourhood of Le Cateau, and rearguards were ordered to be clear of the Maubeuge-Bavai-Eth Road by 5.30 a.m.

'Two cavalry brigades, with the Divisional Cavalry of the II Corps, covered the movement of the II Corps. The remainder of the Cavalry

---

10. Thence they marched to Condé.

Division with the 19th Brigade, the whole under the command of General Allenby, covered the west flank.

'The 4th Division commenced its detrainment at Le Cateau on Sunday, the 23rd, and by the morning of the 25th eleven battalions and a brigade of artillery with Divisional Staff were available for service.

'I ordered General Snow to move out to take up a position with his right south of Solesmes, his left resting on the Cambrai–Le Cateau road south of La Chaprie. In this position the division rendered great help to the effective retirement of the II and I Corps to the new position.

'Although the troops had been ordered to occupy the Cambrai–Le Cateau–Landrecies position, and the ground had, during the 25th, been partially prepared and entrenched, I had grave doubts – owing to the information I received as to the accumulating strength of the enemy against me – as to the wisdom of standing there to fight.

'Having regard to the continued retirement of the French on my right, my exposed left flank, the tendency of the enemy's western corps (II) to envelop me, and, more than all, the exhausted condition of the troops, I determined to make a great effort to continue the retreat till I could put some substantial obstacle, such as the Somme or the Oise, between my troops and the enemy, and afford the former some opportunity of rest and reorganization. Orders were, therefore, sent to the Corps Commanders to continue their retreat as soon as they possibly could towards the general line Vermand–St. Quentin–Ribemont.

'The cavalry, under General Allenby, were ordered to cover the retirement.

'Throughout the 25th, and far into the evening, the I Corps continued its march on Landrecies, following the road along the eastern border of the Forêt de Mormal, and arrived at Landrecies about 10 o'clock. I had intended that the corps should come farther west so as to fill up the gap between Le Cateau and Landrecies, but the men were exhausted and could not get further in without rest.

'The enemy, however, would not allow them this rest, and about 9.30 p.m. a report was received that the 4th Guards Brigade in Landrecies was heavily attacked by troops of the 9th German Army Corps who were coming through the forest on the north of the town. This brigade fought most gallantly, and caused the enemy to suffer tremendous loss in issuing from the forest into the narrow streets of the town. This loss has been estimated from reliable sources at from 700 to 1,000. At the same time

II.A.K.

Denain

IV.

K.K.Marwitz

Kana

Douchy

Bouchain

Noyelles

Somme

Selle

Avesnes le Sec

Saulzoir

Paillencourt

Thun Leveque

Villers en Cauchies

Haussy

Thun St Martin

II.A.K.

Naves

Avesnes

St Vaast

Cagnoncles

St Hilaire

Solesm

Carnières

IV.R.K.

Quiévy

CAMBRAI

Boussières

K.K.Marwitz

Briastre

Caffenières

Bethencourt

Seranvillers

Wambaix

Beauvois

4.engl.Div.

Caudry

IV.

Jnchy

Crèvecoeur

Esnes

II.engl.A.K.

Troi

Ligny

Bertry

Honnechy

1 : 200 000.

10 km

Sebourg

ultain

Eth

gies

Préseau

Wargnies le Grand

St Waast

IX.A.K.

Jenlain

Bavai

Rhonelle

Wargnies le Petit

III.A.K.

auchgnies

Le Quesnoy

F o r ê t

Louvignies

leuville

Aulnoye

d e

in

Englefontaine

Berlaimont

Vendegies

Sassegnies

½IV.A.K.

M o r m a l

Robersart

IX.A.K.

Bousies

la Sambre

orest

Maroilles

Pommereuil

Landrecies

 y

Kanal

Erläuterung.

feau

Vormarsch am 25.8.

.K.

„   „ 26.8

Engl.-franz. Stellungen
am 26.8.

Catillon

I.engl.A.K.

ny

information reached me from Sir Douglas Haig that his 1st Division was also heavily engaged south and east of Maroilles. I sent urgent messages to the commander of the two French Reserve Divisions on my right to come up to the assistance of the I Corps, which they eventually did. Partly owing to this assistance, but mainly to the skilful manner in which Sir Douglas Haig extricated his corps from an exceptionally difficult position in the darkness of the night, they were able at dawn to resume their march south towards Wassigny-on-Guise.

'By about 6 p.m. the II Corps had got into position with their right on Le Cateau, their left in the neighbourhood of Caudry, and the line of defence was continued thence by the 4th Division towards Seranvillers, the left being thrown back.'

These were normal measures demanded by the circumstances, but the chief factor that enabled the British Army to escape was that the German First Army lacked the effective means of making it stand and fight – namely, the three divisions which composed Marwitz's Cavalry Corps. The change of command having taken place when it was on the march Ath–Schelde–Courtrai, this corps did not come under the direct orders of the First Army till the evening of the 24th, and even though the right flank of the First Army was constantly being kept back for the purpose, the Cavalry Corps was unable to accomplish its task of first taking the British Army in flank and then getting behind it.

The Army Order issued from Soignies at 8.30 p.m. on the 24th had to count on the British Army accepting battle on the line Maubeuge–Bavai–Valenciennes. The Order was based on this assumption, and after giving the directions already referred to, ran as follows:

'4. The IV Corps will attack between the Canal de l'Escaut and the Rhonelle stream, silencing the batteries of Fort Curgies; the III Corps, co-operating with it, will move with its left wing by La Bouverie–Blaugies–Bellignies–St. Waast. Both these corps will be across a line Onaing-Angre-Athis by 5 a.m. The IX Corps will cover the attack on Maubeuge, and part of the left wing of the III Corps, according to the extent of its advance, will co-operate in the attack on Bavai. The II Corps will advance tomorrow through the Forest of Raismes, and will get sufficiently south of Valenciennes to enable it to attack the flank of the enemy's position. It will cross the Somain-Raismes railway at 6 a.m.

'5. The IV Reserve Corps will march by Basècles and Blaton tomorrow and arrive at Condé with its advanced guard at 9 a.m., when it will be at the disposal of the Army Commander.

'6. The II Cavalry Corps (Marwitz) will advance south of Denain towards the rear of the British position, and cut the British line of retreat westwards.

'7. Forts Maulde and Flines are to be silenced and kept under fire by the II Corps, so that the later advance of the IV Reserve Corps will not be interfered with by them.

'8. Army Headquarters will move from Soignies to about east of Condé at 10 a.m. on the 25th. A company of the IV Reserve Corps will report there for duty at 11 a.m. Reports will be sent by telephone to Soignies up to 10 a.m. At 11 a.m. representatives of all the corps, except the III Reserve Corps, will call for orders at Thivencelle, east of Condé.

'(*Signed*) von Kluck.'

The outflanking of the left of the British Army, on the assumption that it remained in position, appeared to be guaranteed by the combined efforts of Marwitz's cavalry mass and General von Linsingen's II Corps. The IV Corps, under General Sixt von Armin, the III Corps, under General von Lochow, and part of General von Quast's IX Corps, were to press forward against the British front, whilst the remainder of the IX Corps watched Maubeuge, keeping in touch with the VII Corps of the Second Army. The whole of the IV Reserve Corps, under General von Gronau, was ready in the course of the day, and most of it even earlier, to be employed to west, south, or east, as General Reserve of the Army Commander. The mobility of the Army as shown by its wonderful marching feats was further improved by the excellent measures adopted by the corps commanders.

At 2 a.m. on the 25th an important air report arrived: enemy columns of all arms were in retreat on the roads Bellignies–Bavai, La Flamengrie–Bavai, and Gommegnies–Bavai. The direction in which the movement was being made beyond Bavai had not yet been determined; nevertheless, the Army Commander began to suspect that the British were withdrawing on Maubeuge. At 8.15 a.m. the Army was ordered to advance in a more southerly direction, the II Corps to the line Le Cateau and west of it, the IV Corps to Pommereuil and Landrecies, and the III Corps to Maroilles and Berlaimont. The last-named was also to cover the west and south-west front of Maubeuge, whilst the IX Corps invested the north-west front.

In the course of the morning, however, that appreciation of the situation proved to be wrong, and it appeared that the enemy was withdrawing strong forces through Bavai towards Le Cateau, and smaller detachments through Solesmes in a south-westerly direction. To bring him to a standstill, in addition to the order already mentioned to Marwitz's Cavalry Corps, to bar the retreat of the enemy's columns, the following operation orders were issued from Thivencelle, east of Condé, at 12.15 p.m.:

'The IV Corps is given the Valenciennes–Solesmes–Le Cateau road in addition to those already allotted to it; the II Corps will advance west of this road and as far south as possible; the III Corps is relieved of the duty of watching Maubeuge, and, moving with its main force on its right wing, will march if possible to beyond Maroilles; the IX Corps will take over the covering of these movements from both the north-west and south-west fronts of Maubeuge, and for this purpose will extend its right flank, conforming to the advance of the III Corps, up to the Sambre about Aulnoye. It will make preparations to cross the Sambre, so as to be able to continue its advance later in a southerly direction outside the range of the fortress artillery.'

During the day Marwitz's Cavalry Corps drove back the French territorial troops at Bouchain and Denain and forced the British columns which were retiring in a north-westerly direction from Solesmes on Cambrai, to turn off southwards. The IV Corps was able to attack the British troops at Solesmes, but they did not evacuate the village till after nightfall, after putting up an obstinate resistance. The Second Army this day reached the district between north-east of Avesnes and Chimay.

Army Headquarters at Thivencelle, as has already been mentioned, was guarded by an infantry company. This company was fired at from behind some hedgerows in the immediate neighbourhood of Army Headquarters. The culprits were at once shot, and their houses and belongings burnt. At 6 p.m. the Army Commander drove from his headquarters at Thivencelle to Condé, passing over the half-destroyed bridges of the fortress, and then through Valenciennes (which was friendly), Querenaing and Vendegies (which was burning, the flames coming unpleasantly near the motors, filled up as they were with petrol); thence to north of Solesmes, immediately behind the front of the 8th Division of the IV Corps, where there was still fighting, lively skirmishes taking place in the semi-darkness. It had been thought that Solesmes would be a suitable place for Army Headquarters as soon as it had been occupied by our troops. After the lights of the long column of motors had been put out, and the cars with difficulty turned, the Staff found billets and straw to sleep on late in the evening at Haussy, two miles north of Solesmes. The only comfortable bed which could be found was allotted to the Army Commander. The French peasants were terrified, but became somewhat reassured later.

Army Headquarters were thus up at the front in the very centre of the Army. By the evening of the 25th the leading troops had reached the following line: II Corps and Cavalry Corps, Bouchain–Saulzoir; IV Corps, Solesmes–Bousies–Landrecies; III Corps, Maroilles–Aulnoye; IX Corps, Pont-sur-Sambre–Bavai–Havay in a semi-circle south, west, and north of Maubeuge; IV Reserve Corps, Valenciennes, The corps fronts faced south-west and south-east, meeting at Landrecies.

The Army Order issued from Haussy at 11.50 p.m. on the 25th announced that the First Army would be called on to do another long march in pursuit of the retreating enemy. The II Corps was to march through Cambrai towards Bapaume, advancing west of the road Valenciennes–Vendegies–Villers-en-Cauchies–Cattenières to the high ground about Graincourt, south-west of Cambrai; the IV Reserve Corps, making an early start, was to march by Vendegies and Villers-en-Cauchies to Cattenières; the IV Corps was to move from Solesmes and Landrecies through Caudry and Montay–Caullery–Walincourt to Vendhuille; the III Corps was allotted the Landrecies–Le Cateau road, and was to march by it as far as Maretz; the IX Corps was to protect the communications of the Army from the west and south-west fronts of Maubeuge, and any balance of the corps was to march in rear of the III Corps through Berlaimont and Maroilles to Landrecies. The road Ghissignies–Gommegnies–Villereau-east of Le Quesnoy to Englefontaine was allotted for use by the columns and trains of the III Corps. Representatives of the different corps would receive orders about noon at Solesmes, where Army Headquarters would move to from Haussy on the morning of the 26th.

The Memorandum may speak for itself regarding the course of the operations during the 26th:

'The bitter fighting which developed on this day between Cambrai and Le Cateau on the front Crèvecoeur–Reumont formed the crisis of the several days' fighting in pursuit of the British, which has been collectively termed the 'Battle of Solesmes.'[11] Early in the morning Marwitz's Cavalry Corps attacked through Wambaix–Beauvois–Quievy against the enemy retreating in a westerly direction,[12] forcing part of the hostile force southwards, and holding it till the advanced guards of the infantry corps arrived on the scene. The IV Corps engaged strong British forces[13] on the front Caudry–Troisville–Reumont at about 9 a.m., and got into a difficult position against a well-entrenched enemy.[14] The IV Reserve Corps was therefore ordered to make an outflanking attack against the northern wing of this position, and the III Corps a similar attack against its southern flank.[15]

'The former corps, however, came up against French troops near Cattenières,[16] and the latter corps, ordered to march on Maretz, did not get farther than Honnechy on the 26th, so that the attempted outflanking operation was not effective. By evening the IV Reserve Corps had succeeded in forcing back its opponent in a southerly direction,[17] whilst the IV Corps[18] drove in the right flank of the British position. The II Corps beat back strong French forces at Cambrai.[19]

---

11. See Note 2, p. 59.
12. The British were not retreating on the morning of the 26th, and made no movement westwards.
13. Two divisions of the II Corps, which the III German Corps also attacked.
14. The entrenchments made by the British were of the most hasty description. Some had been dug in the right and centre by the inhabitants; they provided only the scantiest cover, and in some cases, to avoid damage to crops, were so sited as to be useless and dangerous.
15. The British position in fact ran east and west.
16. According to the narrative of Captain Wirth quoted below, there were no French troops on the left of the 4th (British) Division so far east as this at the time of the attack of the IV Reserve Corps. German cavalry driven back by the 4th Division were there. He distinctly states that the 7th Reserve Division attacked the British.
17. The IV Reserve Corps' account does not agree with this; its attack got no farther than Wambaix (*vide* narrative of Captain Wirth, 7th Reserve Division Staff, in 'Von der Saale zur Aisne').
18. With the assistance of the III Corps.

A cavalry patrol entered Lille without meeting any opposition. Strong enemy forces retired during the 26th in front of the Second Army from Landrecies and Avesnes towards Guise and Vervins. On the 27th the Second Army was to continue the pursuit, its right wing marching by Leval, Landrecies, and Catillon on St. Quentin.

The Second Army Commander ordered that Maubeuge should be invested by two of his own divisions and one division of the First Army. First Army Headquarters were, however, of the opinion that one or two reserve divisions would be quite sufficient for the investment of the fortress, which was garrisoned only by indifferent troops: it therefore passed on the order of the Second Army Commander to the Supreme Command, and at the same time asked whether the subordination of the First Army to the Second Army Commander was to remain in force. Thereupon the Supreme Command released the First Army, making it independent of the Second Army Commander, and decided that the Second Army should invest Maubeuge with its own troops alone.

According to the reports received, the whole British Expeditionary Force, consisting of six infantry divisions and one cavalry division, in addition to several French Territorial divisions, was in front of the First Army.[20] On the 26th August more than 2,600 prisoners, mostly British, 7 field batteries, and one heavy battery of artillery were taken by the First Army.[21] If the British held their ground on the 27th, the enveloping movement round both flanks by the II and III Corps[22] respectively might bring about another considerable victory.

Let us now turn to the despatch of Sir John French on the operations during these days of the Battle of Solesmes:

---

19. The rearguard of the 84th Territorial Division.
20. Actually three British infantry divisions (3rd, 4th, and 5th), the 19th Infantry Brigade, the 84th French Territorial Division, and Sordêt's French Cavalry Corps, fought at Le Cateau, and the British cavalry was hardly engaged.
21. The British lost 38 guns, including only one 60-pounder gun, not battery. The French lost no guns (see Major Becke's 'The Royal Regiment of Artillery at Le Cateau').
22. Von Kluck ignores the presence of the I (British) Corps on the east of his III Corps, and the French Territorial Divisions from Bapaume and Arras outside his II Corps.

'During the fighting on the 24th and 25th the cavalry became a good deal scattered, but by the early morning of the 26th General Allenby had succeeded in concentrating two brigades to the south of Cambrai.

'The 4th Division was placed under the orders of the General Officer Commanding the Second Army Corps.

'On the 24th the French Cavalry Corps, consisting of three divisions, under General Sordêt, had been in billets north of Avesnes. On my way back from Bavai, which was my "Poste de Commandement" during the fighting of the 23rd and 24th, I visited General Sordêt, and earnestly requested his co-operation and support. He promised to obtain sanction from his Army Commander to act on my left flank, but said that his horses were too tired to move before the next day. Although he rendered me valuable assistance later on in the course of the retirement, he was unable for the reasons given to afford me any support on the most critical day of all – viz., the 26th.

'At daybreak it became apparent that the enemy was throwing the bulk of his strength against the left of the position occupied by the II Corps and the 4th Division.

'At this time the guns of four German Army Corps were in position against them, and Sir Horace Smith-Dorrien reported to me that he judged it impossible to continue his retirement at daybreak (as ordered) in face of such an attack.

'I sent him orders to use his utmost endeavours to break off the action and retire at the earliest possible moment, as it was impossible for me to send him any support, the I Corps being at the moment incapable of movement.

'The French Cavalry Corps, under General Sordêt, was coming up on our left rear early in the morning, and I sent an urgent message to him to do his utmost to come up and support the retirement of my left flank; but, owing to the fatigue of his horses, he found himself unable to intervene in any way.

'There had been no time to entrench the position properly, but the troops showed a magnificent front to the terrible fire which confronted them.

'The artillery, although outmatched by at least four to one, made a splendid fight, and inflicted heavy losses on their opponents.

'At length it became apparent that, if complete annihilation was to be avoided, a retirement must be attempted; and the order was given to commence it about 3.30 p.m. The movement was covered with the most devoted intrepidity and determination by the artillery, which had itself suffered heavily, and the fine work done by the cavalry in the further retreat from the position assisted materially in the final completion of this most difficult and dangerous operation.

'Fortunately the enemy had himself suffered too heavily to engage in an energetic pursuit.

'I cannot close the brief account of this glorious stand of the British troops without putting on record my deep appreciation of the valuable services rendered by General Sir Horace Smith-Dorrien.

'I say without hesitation that the saving of the left wing of the Army under my command on the morning of the 26th August could never have been accomplished unless a commander of rare and unusual coolness, intrepidity, and determination had been present to personally conduct the operation.

'The retreat was continued far into the night of the 26th and through the 27th and 28th, on which date the troops halted on the line Noyon–Chauny–La Fère, having then thrown off the weight of the enemy's pursuit.

'On the 27th and 28th I was much indebted to General Sordêt and the French Cavalry Division which he commands for materially assisting my retirement and successfully driving back some of the enemy on Cambrai.

'General d'Amade also, with the 61st and 62nd French Reserve Divisions, moved down from the neighbourhood of Arras on the enemy's right flank and took much pressure off the rear of the British forces.

'This closes the period covering the heavy fighting which commenced at Mons on Sunday afternoon, 23rd August, and which really constituted a four days' battle.'

By the evening of the 26th the First Army, after its heavy fighting with the British and French, had gained ground as follows: On the right, Marwitz's Cavalry Corps had occupied the district west of Cambrai; Von Linsingen's II Corps, pressing forward incessantly through Cambrai, had reached Hermies–Marcoing; Von Gronau's IV Reserve Corps arrived at Crèvecoeur after a prodigious march from Valenciennes through Cattenières; farther to the left, the IV Corps reached the line Caudry–Troisvilles–Reumont; the III Corps reached Honnechy with its advanced troops, and the IX Corps arrived at the Sambre crossings at

Landrecies. The Army had thus made a considerable advance with its right wing with constant fighting; at the same time, it had kept touch with the Second Army.

During the day the operation staff of Army Headquarters had hurried from Solesmes to the front of the 8th Division (Lieut.-General Hildebrand) in the area Quievy–Viesly, in the hottest part of the battle in that neighbourhood, which offered the welcome opportunity of watching the local fighting and also of meeting General Sixt von Armin and General Hildebrand. The Army Commander still hoped to be able to outflank the British on both wings. The Chief of the Staff and his Deputy received a generous but harmless baptism of fire during this visit to the front, and the Army Commander was honoured by a British shrapnel, which burst between him and three members of his Staff without doing any damage. It seemed unnecessary to go any closer to the front line.

After returning to Solesmes, operation orders for the 27th were issued from Army Headquarters at 9.13 p.m. As constant reports were coming in that the enemy was in retreat, the II Corps was ordered to advance at 2 a.m. from Hermies towards Manancourt and from Marcoing towards Guyencourt, north of Villers Faucon, in order to continue the attack on the enemy, presumably retreating, wherever he was met. The IV Reserve Corps (Von Gronau) was to advance in the gap between the II and the IV Corps. The IV Corps (Sixt von Armin) was allotted as zone of manoeuvre the areas Caudry-Ligny-Walincourt-Vendhuille and Reumont–Serain–Bellicourt. The III Corps (Von Lochow) was to move to south of the IV Corps beyond Maretz, which it had been unable to reach the day before. A line roughly Esnes–Caudry–Reumont was to be passed at 5 a.m.[23] The leading division of the IX Corps (Von Quast), marching by Landrecies, was to arrive with the heavy corps artillery at Le Cateau at 10 a.m., where it would be at the disposal of the Army Commander; its other division was to be left opposite the west front of Maubeuge. Marwitz's Cavalry Corps was to advance in front of the II Corps and hinder the enemy's retreat.'[24] There were thus on the right and left wings of the First Army two almost

---

23. This seems a fairly late start for the pursuit, as the action was broken off at 3 p.m. As Sir John French wrote in his first despatch: 'The enemy had himself suffered too heavily to engage in an energetic pursuit.'

equally strong fighting groups in touch with one another, which would put the necessary vigour into the pursuit. Army Headquarters remained in Solesmes.

The retreat of the enemy in a westerly direction north of the Somme appeared to have been prevented by the timely pressure of the right wing of the First Army.[25] When the latter crossed the Somme, probably within the next forty-eight hours, there would be an attractive prospect 'of throwing back the enemy's left wing on to the strong French forces retreating southwards in front of the Second Army.' During the pursuit on the 27th several successful isolated encounters took place with portions of the army of General d'Amade, which had been recently formed near Amiens, to cover the left flank of the British Army. Thus at Guyencourt the II Corps drove back the French 3rd Cavalry Division;[26] at Dailly, French Reserve Regiments were encountered; and at Bus, Marwitz's Cavalry Corps met the French 84th Territorial Division.

During its fourteen days' offensive from Aix-la-Chapelle to near Peronne the First Army had now completed two-thirds of the wheel through Brussels on Paris. The requirements of the strategic situation made it impossible to give any rest days in the true sense of the word. Marches and fights, battles and marches, followed one another without interval. All the more urgent, therefore, was the need for incessant care of the lines of communication, so as to ensure their safety as well as a regular supply of food and ammunition. On the 24th August the area of the Lines of Communication Command was moved forward to a line Ninove–Hal–Waterloo, and a garrison for Hal provided; in addition, the chief places on the lines of communication were ordered to be put into a state of defence, by barbed-wire entanglements, and the erection of suitable buildings, while all necessary bridges and railheads were put in hand. To assist in guarding the communications, seven battalions and two squadrons of *Landsturm* troops were brought from Magdeburg on that day.

---

24. This misdirection of the cavalry kept it away from the British. It was opposed by General Sordêt's Cavalry Corps' with considerable success.
25. No retreat westwards was ever contemplated. Von Kluck still seems to think that the B.E.F. was based on Calais.
26. This belonged to General Sordêt's Cavalry Corps, not to General d'Amade's forces.

The IX Reserve Corps reached Tongres, north of Liège, on the 25th. In conjunction with the III Reserve Corps and some *Landwehr* troops which were expected shortly, it was to take over the duty of observing the Antwerp garrison: this combined investing force was under the command of General von Beseler. It was hoped that the Supreme Command would now hurry forward the brigade of the IV Reserve Corps which was still back in Brussels, so as to enable the unsupported and open right flank of the First Army to be maintained at full fighting strength. Repeated applications for this had not yet been complied with. A further request for the addition of heavy artillery to this weakened corps was made. Troops were ordered to take the utmost care to husband their ammunition and to make a special point of picking up any left on the battlefields. In view of the possible interference with passing supply columns by the population or by isolated detachments of the enemy, all the men with the transport columns and trains were given rifles, a precaution already advocated in peace time. The communications between the corps and Lines of Communication Headquarters were further improved on the 27th, and by request of the former the railways leading to Paris were reconnoitred and any rolling-stock found on them examined. The Deputy Chief of the Staff and his General Staff Officer, Von dem Hagen, who had been associated with the Army Commander when Inspector-General of the Eighth Army District, and whose excellent qualifications were well known to him, supervised all the lines of communication matters mentioned above in a most thorough and far-seeing manner, in order to expand and strengthen the vital artery of the Army. The offensive wheel through the lands of the Flemings and the Walloons towards the Somme and Picardy which had fallen to the lot of the First Army could now be continued with complete confidence, in view of the successes gained and the abundant reinforcements expected, thanks also to its excellent troops and their thoroughly reliable leaders, both in the senior and junior ranks.

With admirable foresight the Chief of the Staff of the Army issued instructions to the various corps regarding the importance of the Somme line in their immediate vicinity, as also of the section of the Oise below La Fère. The valley of the river and the canal of the Somme forms a considerable obstacle below Peronne. This double obstacle, in places fifteen yards broad, is interrupted by swampy ponds and meadows, covered with undergrowth. The high ground lies well back on the northern bank, so that artillery fire from it on to the southern bank would not be sufficiently effective; nevertheless its occupation as soon as possible was important. The fortifications of Peronne were obsolete, but they might be useful on emergency; the bed of the river widens out like a lake as it passes the town, and the old castle, where Louis XI was captured by Charles of Burgundy in 1468, is well adapted for a stubborn local defence. The obsolete fort of La Fère might have artillery in it; the section of the Oise below it is very important from a military point of view. From La Fère to Chauny an attack against the high ground along the southern left bank would be difficult, though below Chauny the high ground on the northern right bank commands the flat country on the opposite side of the river. Between Noyon and Rivecourt, below Compiègne, the thickly wooded right bank overlooks a wide stretch of country, whilst the woods on the left bank, situated away from the river and the canal, together with those of Carlepont, Laigue, and Compiègne, might make a defence of that area very difficult. The Oise, which varies from six to fifteen feet in depth, is thirty yards broad at La Fère, increasing to fifty yards at Compiègne, and to one hundred yards at its junction with the Seine. The Oise Canal, which accompanies the river from La Fère down to Janville, above Compiègne, is twenty-four yards broad as far as Chauny, and from there to the junction twenty-eight yards broad; the breadth at the locks is six and a half yards.

On the 27th August, after the day's fighting, the Army stood in two groups ready to attack the Somme position. The II Corps, echeloned behind the Cavalry Corps, was east of Combles near Sailly Saillisel–Manancourt; the IV Reserve Corps was at Villers Faucon; the IV Corps was west of Vendhuille, and the III Corps at Nauroy; the leading troops of the IX Corps were back at Busigny, north of Bohain. The Second Army was to advance, its right wing moving by Catillon, south-east of Le Cateau, through Bohain towards St. Quentin.

In the Army Order issued at Solesmes that evening at 8.15 p.m. the Somme crossings were allotted as follows:

II Corps, Bray and westwards, inclusive of Corbie;
IV Reserve Corps, Cappy and Eclusier;
IV Corps, Feuillères, Clery, and Peronne;

III Corps, Brie and St. Christ;

IX Corps, Epenancourt, Falvy, and Bethancourt.

Corps were to march by the following roads:

II Corps, Combles–Montauban–west of Maricourt–Bray, and roads to
westwards;

IV Reserve Corps, Fins–Manancourt–south-east side of Combles–
Maurepas–south-east side of Maricourt;

IV Corps, Lieramont–Moislains–Clery and Villers Faucon–Peronne;

III Corps, Hargiert–Roisel–Hancourt–Cartigny–Brie and La Verguier–
Vendelles–Pceuvilly–Estrée-en-Chaussée–Athies–St. Christ;

IX Corps will reach Pontru with its advanced guard, marching by
Premont–Brancourt–Joncourt–Belleenglise.

The corps were to keep close on the heels of the retreating enemy with their
cavalry and field batteries, so as to increase his general disorder and be able
to attack him at the Somme crossings.[27] The cavalry of the III Corps was to
secure the crossings at Falvy and Bethancourt for the IX Corps, in addition
to reconnoitring its own line of march through Nesle and Ham. The IX
Corps was to patrol out to its left flank beyond St. Quentin towards Jussy
and La Fère, and get into touch with the right flank of the Second Army.
The Cavalry Corps was to advance across the Somme west of Peronne
and hold the river crossings open for the Army. It was also to reconnoitre
up to the Oise and towards Amiens. The 18th Pioneer Regiment was to
accompany the IV Corps and be temporarily under its orders.

Air reconnaissances were to be made by the II Corps in the triangle
Albert–Doullens–Amiens, by the IV Corps in the area Bray–Amiens–
Montdidier, by the III Corps in the area Bray–Montdidier–Nesle–
Peronne, and by the IX Corps in the sector between Ham, Noyon, and La
Fère. Army Headquarters were to be at Solesmes up to noon on the 28th,
when they would move to Villers Faucon.

By these orders the Army Commander hoped to be able to outflank the
Somme salient from north and east by pushing forward his right wing

---

27. Fortunately the corps did nothing of the kind. The British retreat from Le
Cateau was practically unmolested.

and thus force the crossings, with the II Corps at Bray and Corbie, the IV Reserve Corps and the Cavalry Corps above Bray and downstream from Peronne, the IV Corps at Peronne, the III Corps above the bend of the Somme at Brie and St. Christ, and the IX Corps, coming up on the following day, at Falvy and Bethancourt.

On the morning of the 28th the Cavalry Corps was surprised in its billets by the French 61st and 62nd Reserve Divisions. The French, however, were routed from the field at Manancourt by parts of the II and IV Reserve Corps. Other units of the II and IV Reserve Corps, the latter being completely deployed, forced back strong enemy forces,[28] with heavy loss, in a westerly direction from the front Sailly Saillisel–Morval – that is to say, in the direction of march ordered for the II Corps on the right wing, through Combles. For reasons not yet understood, the II Corps moved away from its own line of advance towards the crossings which had been allotted to the IV Reserve Corps, so that the latter had to continue its advance behind instead of on the left of the II Corps. The war diaries of these two corps will throw further light on this matter.

The intention of the Army Commander to use a corps reinforced with heavy artillery as a strong right wing had reluctantly to be abandoned.

The III Corps repulsed several battalions which tried to advance from St. Quentin and also drove back the French 3rd Cavalry Division. By evening, after short though frequently severe encounters, the left bank of the Somme from Feuillieres to St. Christ was in German possession. In front of this line stood the French 3rd and 5th Cavalry Divisions and roughly eight infantry battalions, mostly Reserve Alpine Chasseurs. It was understood that further French forces were to be detrained near Amiens and south of it.

On the morning of the 29th Army Headquarters moved to Peronne, which had been taken by the IV Corps.

During the afternoon of the 28th a wireless message was received at Army Headquarters at Villers Faucon from His Majesty the Commander-in-Chief which ran as follows: 'The First Army is today approaching the heart of France in its victorious march, after winning rapid and decisive victories against the Belgians, the British, and the French. I congratulate the Army on its brilliant successes, and wish to express my imperial gratitude.'

---

28. The 61st and 62nd Reserve Divisions mentioned above.

At this period the Headquarters of the First Army summed up the situation as follows: 'The left wing of the main French forces is retreating in a southerly and south-westerly direction in front of the victorious Second and Third Armies. It appears to be of decisive importance to find the flank of this force, whether retreating or in position, force it away from Paris, and outflank it. Compared with this new objective, the attempt to force the British Army away from the coast is of minor importance.'[29]

At midday on the 28th, on the basis of this appreciation, it was proposed to the Commander of the Second Army that a wheel inwards should be made by the two Armies towards the Oise, the First Army moving on Compiègne-Noyon, and the Second Army with its right flank on Quierzy and Chauny. During that evening, however, a communication arrived from the Supreme Command entitled 'General Directions for the Further Conduct of the Operations.' It expected renewed opposition by the French and British forces on the Aisne, with their left wing advanced abreast of a line St. Quentin–La Fère–Laon, also later on the Marne, with the left flank resting on Paris. A concentration of fresh forces on the lower Seine was also considered possible. An immediate advance of the German Armies on Paris was to prevent the French Army getting any rest and stop the formation of fresh concentrations. 'The First Army, with the II Cavalry Corps under its orders, will march west of the Oise towards the lower Seine. It must be prepared to co-operate in the fighting of the Second Army. It will also be responsible for the protection of the right flank of the Armies, and will take steps to prevent any new enemy concentration in its zone of operations.[30]

'The Second Army, with the I Cavalry Corps under its orders, will advance across the line Laon–La Fère towards Paris. It will also invest and capture Maubeuge and later La Fère, as also Laon in co-operation with the Third Army.

'All the Armies will mutually co-operate with one another and support each other during the fighting. The strong resistance which is expected to be met on the Aisne and later on the Marne may necessitate a wheel inwards of the Armies from a south-westerly to a southerly direction.'

---

29. Still the idea that the B.E.F. was based on Calais and ports near it.
30. The First Army failed, as will be seen, to prevent the concentration of General Maunoury's Army north-east of Paris.

These directions implied that the First Army would continue its advance in a south-westerly direction for the time being. They did not exclude the possibility of a wheel inwards to the south, such as the Army Commander had contemplated, should the general situation make it appear necessary. Information on the general situation of the German Western Army in France such as would have been useful for the guidance of the Commander of the Army on the right flank either was not given or was suppressed: a case in point was the alleged weakening of the Western Army by taking two corps away from the Second Army to be sent to the Eastern theatre of war.[31] In the opinion of the First Army Commander, the necessary force should have been taken away from the opposite flank of the Armies, which was wheeling up against the line of fortresses in Lorraine, a movement which might well have been discontinued. For the situation in the West was only just reaching its full development, and in order to be prepared for it the transference of several divisions, with, if possible, heavy batteries, from the left wing of the German Armies would have been welcomed, in order to form an echelon behind the right wing.

A decisive battle would have to be fought in France in the near future in order to enable sufficient help to be sent to East and West Prussia. The postponement of the mobilization of the Armies for three days for political reasons could only be made good by rapidity of movement and by concentrating the massed strength of the Armies in the decisive area.

The directions quoted above did not admit of any slowing down of the operations of the First Army and a good rest could not therefore be given to the long-suffering troops. The message of appreciation sent by the Emperor, however, spurred on all those taking part in the campaign to fresh efforts, and the marches on the two following days were fortunately only of moderate length. The health of the troops was most carefully watched by officers of all grades, so that their marching capacity was kept up to a high pitch of excellence. The travelling kitchens were an invaluable asset in this respect, and brought up plenty of nourishing food at every long halt or resting-place. The truth of Field-Marshal Count Haeseler's

---

31. Actually, the Guard Reserve Corps was taken from the Second Army, and the XI Corps and 8th Cavalry Division from the Third Army.

words was established that 'both man and horse are capable of amazing achievements in war.'

The history of the war further confirms this. From the various French authorities so far available, it appears that the enemy, retreating with heavy fighting day and night, was in a state of extreme depression.

To sum up: the occupation of the Somme area marked the conclusion of the fighting with the British Army for the time being. In spite of the great efforts of the First Army, the British had escaped the repeated attempts to envelop them. They continued their retreat southwards. The Army of General d'Amade was surprised while still in the act of concentrating, and a considerable part of it had been dispersed.[32] As in the fighting against the Belgian Army, so in the operations against the Armies of General French and General d'Amade, rapidity of advance and immediate attack had been the decisive factors. By these means, co-operation between the Belgians, British, and French had been prevented; each had been taken in detail while still deploying, and defeated.[33] The despatch of General French shows clearly the embarrassed state of his Army, as also that of his Allies.[34] This gallant British Army, with such excellent fighting qualities, had to change its base from the Channel ports to St. Nazaire on the coast of Brittany. With luck Calais would come into German possession, provided troops from another part of the Western theatre could be set free for the purpose.

* * *

Note 1: Commencing for convenience on the left, the Allied forces at Mons were as follows : In Condé, the French 84th Territorial Division;

---

32. General Maunoury took over from General d'Amade on the 27th August. The French 61st and 62nd Reserve Divisions, which formed part of his Army, had been attacked (see p. 55), but not dispersed.
33. The British who fought with French on each side of them from Mons onward had hardly been taken in detail, still less defeated.
34. Nothing to this effect can be found in the despatch. Field-Marshal French says, writing of events up to the 30th September: 'We were not severely pressed by the enemy.'

next to this, along the Canal, the British 19th Infantry Brigade. These were not attacked on the 23rd August. Then came the British 5th Division, which, according to the German General Staff Monograph, *Die Schlacht bei Mons,* was attacked by the 8th and 7th German Divisions, and part of the 5th Division. Next on the right was the British 3rd Division, holding a salient round Mons as far south-east as Villers Ghislain. This Division was attacked by three and a half German divisions, viz., part of the 5th, the 6th, 18th and 17th. The British I Corps, which extended the line farther south-eastwards to Peissant, was only attacked by artillery, covered by the 16th Dragoons. The British Cavalry Division was in rear of the left flank, and was not in action on the 23rd; the 5th Cavalry Brigade was in advance of the British right flank.

Note 2: The British Battle of Le Cateau; the official German title (vide *Schlachten und Gefechte*) is Solesmes-Le Cateau. The Allied forces engaged were, from right to left: II Corps (5th and 3rd Divisions), with the 19th Infantry Brigade, its right in Le Cateau; the 4th Division, its left on Esnes. There was then a gap in the front line to Cambrai, covered by Sordêt's Cavalry Corps and British 4th Cavalry Brigade. Through Cambrai and west of it the French 84th Territorial Division was slowly retiring, with the 61st and 62nd Reserve Divisions, which had come up from Arras and Bapaume, still farther west. The British I Corps was about seven miles east of the II Corps, and not engaged in the battle. Connection between the two Corps was kept by the 2nd and 3rd Cavalry Brigades.

Chapter 3

The Inward Wheel Against the Enemy's Main Forces – Paris – Crossing the Marne

On the 29th August the First Army, now in possession of the bend of the Somme, moved forward towards the Avre, a tributary of the Somme, and the fighting against the Army of General d'Amade became more extended. The IV Reserve Corps, which at this time was in a dangerous situation, was near Combles covering the right flank of the Army from the area Arras–Amiens, and the II Corps was engaged in heavy fighting near Proyart. The IV Corps and the Cavalry Corps were occupied with a less severe encounter on the line Rosières–Meharicourt against strong detachments of the French VII Corps and Alpine Chasseurs. The enemy was thrown back along the whole front and pursued well into the night of the 30th August by the II Corps as far as Villers Bretonneux. The IV Reserve Corps reported strong forces in bivouac near Albert and was about to attack a position close by on the Ancre stream, but found it evacuated by the enemy.s

The detrainment of more troops was reported at Amiens, Moreuil, and south of it, and Roye and Noyon were found to be occupied. The French Commander-in-Chief was apparently putting in any troops at his disposal, in addition to units withdrawn from other parts of the front, against the First Army. During the next few days the presence of the following units was established: VII Corps, Alpine Chasseurs, 61st and 62nd Reserve Divisions, 81st, 82nd, 84th, and 88th Territorial Divisions, and the 3rd and 5th Cavalry Divisions.[1] It was therefore essential to defeat the enemy before he could gain time to reorganize his masses.

---

1. The German First Army of ten divisions and three cavalry divisions need hardly have feared this force. The VII Corps consisted of the 13th Division and the 63rd Reserve Division.

With this object in view, the attack was to be continued on the 30th August, and an enveloping movement by both flanks was aimed at, the IV Reserve Corps advancing on Amiens and the IX Corps moving round south of Roye supported by Marwitz's Cavalry Corps.

The co-operation of the cavalry was especially needed, as the IX Corps had been considerably weakened through having temporarily to send its 17th Infantry Division to help the Second Army in performing its own special task; for on the evening of the 29th General von Bülow had reported that his Second Army was engaged in hard fighting with a superior enemy on the line Essigny-le-Grand–Mont d'Origny-sur-Oise–Haution. In view of the many needs of the First Army for its own operations and of the calls already made on its fighting strength, such as leaving behind the III Reserve Corps in front of Antwerp, the 43rd Reserve Infantry Brigade of General von Lepel in Brussels, and supplying the necessary troops for the constantly lengthening lines of communication, it had been a difficult request to comply with; nevertheless, the situation being what it was, the sacrifice was unavoidable.[2]

The artillery of the division thus transferred then took part in the battle of the Second Army at St. Quentin,[3] whilst its infantry was employed as reserve behind the right wing of General von Bülow's Army. The heavy artillery of the IX Corps remained with its leading division, the 18tb, about Roye.

By the morning of the 30th it was realized that the Army of General d'Amade[4] was not remaining on our side of the Avre, and the force near Amiens, estimated to be one corps, was retiring in front of the IV Reserve Corps. Information from the Second Army pointed to the fact that the enemy was delivering his main attack against its right flank on St. Quentin. The First Army Commander therefore had to consider the possible necessity of wheeling inwards from a southwesterly to a southerly direction, or even a south-easterly one, should the Second Army need immediate assistance. The left wheel of the First Army which such a situation would demand was prepared for by the Army Order issued at

---

2. Von Kluck had himself proposed this movement (see p. 56).
3. Battle of Guise.
4. General Maunoury, not General d'Amade.

9.30 a.m. on the 30th August. The IV Reserve Corps and the II Corps were to move in the direction Amiens-Moreuil, and the IV, III, and half the IX Corps were to move with the right towards Braches on the Avre above Moreuil and with the left to Roye and south-west of it, the corps thus being in echelon to the left.

At 11.30 a.m. the Army Commander issued further instructions for the march. The IX Corps, less the 17th Infantry Brigade, to march to Guiscard, the III Corps by the road Roye-Noyon, and IV to Roye-sur Matz. The II Corps to protect this flank march from interference from the Avre, and the IV Corps from the direction of Amiens. Thus the movement intended to envelop both the flanks of the retreating enemy had developed into a wheel of the Army to southwards, and thanks to the skilful leading of the corps commanders no difficulties were met with.

At 5.55 p.m. a wireless message arrived from Second Army Headquarters: 'Enemy decisively beaten today; strong forces retiring on La Fère. The British, who were barring the Oise south-west of La Fère, are also retreating in a southerly, and some in a south-easterly, direction.[5] The enemy in front of the Third and Fourth Armies is also in retreat. The Second Army will rest on the 31st August except that the bombardment of the forts of La Fère will be carried out.'

At 6.30 p.m. another wireless message arrived asking for the co-operation of the First Army: 'To gain the full advantages of the victory, a wheel inwards of the First Army pivoted on Chauny towards the line La Fère–Laon is urgently desired.'

The Second Army Commander obviously placed a higher value on the importance and resisting power of La Fère, Laon, and Reims than they proved to deserve. His request, which was contrary to the directions issued by the Supreme Command, could not, in the opinion of the First Army Headquarters, be carried out, although an attempt might be made to take the retreating enemy in flank by an energetic pursuit in a southerly and south-easterly direction. During the evening of the 30th August the Supreme Command was therefore informed that: 'The First Army has wheeled round towards the Oise and will advance on the 31st by Compiègne and Noyon to exploit the success of the Second Army.' On

---

5. This is correct. The I Corps went south, the remainder a little east of south.

the morning of the 31st the answer arrived by wireless: 'The movement begun by the First Army is in accordance with the wishes of the Supreme Command.'

The Marching and Fighting Capacity of the Army
The further course of the campaign was to make the greatest possible demands on the capacity of the transport and supply columns, the life-blood of the Army. It was the constant anxiety of all the commanders to maintain their efficiency. The condition of the draught animals kept satisfactory, thanks to the abundant supply of oats in the fields and the activity shown in conveying it thence to the store depots. Officers and non-commissioned officers, in spite of the great lack of technical knowledge that existed, did all they could to reduce the difficulties of this all-important service. But at the outbreak of the war, the cadres on which to form the Supply Service were wholly inadequate, and it was therefore not surprising that troubles of a discreditable character arose. The wholesale increase of the establishment of train personnel which the General Staff had for years been trying to obtain had not become a fact; the growth of this Service to its present enormous size began only when the hour of mobilization had struck, and of course no corresponding development of organic power was possible. The strictest supervision and most detailed orders were necessary to make up for this lack of organization. As a result of accumulated experience, helped by imagination, it gradually became clear to all that the constant preparedness of the Army and the maintenance of its strength depended to a very great extent on the efficiency and reliability of its trains and supply columns. Herein lies the justification of the enormous demands made on them during these most troublesome and difficult operations. Many points, however, as to the type, structure, and weight of many of the vehicles employed, both horse-drawn and motor-driven, as well as their mobility, will have to undergo a further test.

The 31st August
In pursuance of the decision made on the evening of the 30th and communicated to the Supreme Command, it was impossible to avoid imposing on the troops an even longer march than on the previous days, in spite of their extraordinary efforts in the past weeks. The IV Reserve

Corps was required to reach Ailly with its advanced troops, the II Corps Maignelay and Tricot, the IV Corps the wooded district east of St. Maur and Mareuil, the III Corps Bailly and Cuts, the IX Corps Coucy-le-Château; the 17th Infantry Division was sent forward through Chauny.

During the day it was seen that the enemy was retreating beyond a line Verberie–Vic–Soissons, the French western flank apparently moving by Soissons. The corps had therefore to continue their advance, the advanced guard of the III Corps reaching the lower Aisne about Attichy and Vic. A short stay of First Army Headquarters in Lassigny gave the Army Commander an opportunity of himself witnessing the excellent march discipline of the 5th Division. The IX Corps occupied Vezaponin with its leading troops. Marwitz's Cavalry Corps, leaving the neighbourhood north of Roye-sur-Matz, crossed the Oise at Thourotte, and passing through the Forest of Laigue met the 5th Division, the right column of the III Corps, near Attichy, north of the Aisne. The I Cavalry Corps belonging to the Second Army had arrived at Noyon on the 30th August, and was ordered to advance on the 31st through Ribecourt on the Oise towards Soissons.

Thus on the evening of the 31st the Army stood in two large groups in echelon, the left group in front, consisting of the Corps of Marwitz, Lochow, and Quast, on the lower Aisne; and the right group, consisting of the Corps of Gronau, Linsingen, and Sixt von Armin, echeloned behind from Ailly on the Selle through Maignelay to Moreuil and Lamotte in the woods west of Noyon. The IV Reserve Corps covered the right flank, whilst the cavalry of Bülow's Army protected the left and also kept up communication between the two Armies. First Army Headquarters moved from Peronne to Noyon.

On the 1st September the Army came into close touch with strong enemy rearguards. The Army Order of the previous evening had stated that the western flank of the French Army had retired on the 31st from La Fère through Soissons; the enemy – apparently the British Army – was in retreat from the line of the Oise between Noyon–Verberie through Senlis–Crépy-en-Valois–Villers Cotterêts, whilst a weaker force was withdrawing towards Clermont in front of the II Corps. Another effort was therefore made to attack the British in retreat on the 1st September, and the Army was ordered in a southerly direction as follows:

The IV Reserve to the district north of St. Just-en-Chaussée, covering as before the right flank of the Army and the lines of communication.

The II Corps by Estrées St. Denis and Remy till its leading troops are across the Oise about Verberie and Le Meux. Reconnaissances to be made on the right flank to the line Clermont–Creil–Senlis:

The IV Corps by Compiègne–Gilocourt and by Thourotte–Pierrefonds towards the southern side of the Forest of Compiègne.

The III Corps by Attichy–Taillefontaine and Vic–Vivières.

The IX Corps by Ambleny–Longpont, its 17th Infantry Division marching by Chauny, after having reached St. Simon near the junction of the Crozat Canal with the Somme on the 31st.

The IV, III, and IX Corps were to cross the Aisne and the Oise respectively with their advanced guards at 8 a.m. on the 1st September. Marwitz's Cavalry Corps was to move through Villers Cotterêts against the French flank, whilst the cavalry of the Second Army was ordered to advance through the wooded country between Villers Cotterêts and Soissons.

As a result of these movements, the II Corps, supported by the Cavalry Corps which kept west of the Attichy district, became involved in heavy fighting for the possession of the important Oise crossings at Verberie and St. Sauveur. The IV Corps was in action at Gilocourt late in the afternoon, and the II Corps at Villers Cotterêts.[6] Owing to the fighting at Verberie, Marwitz's Cavalry Corps was unable to reach its objective Nanteuil-le-Haudouin; its 4th Division, after making a successful surprise attack on the enemy's bivouacs at Nery, became seriously engaged with superior forces near Rosières, north of Nanteuil-le-Haudouin, and incurred heavy losses.[7]

---

6. This was the rearguard action fought by the British 4th (Guards) Brigade and 6th Infantry Brigade. The two brigades were opposed, as von Kluck tells us in the opening sentence of this paragraph, by the II Cavalry Corps and II Corps. The fighting lasted from 10 a.m. to 6 p.m., when the British drew off undisturbed.

7. As is notorious the German 4th Cavalry Division left two-thirds of its guns at Nery, and abandoned the others in Ermenonville Wood. The British lost no guns. For the British account of this action see *R.U.S.I. Journal*, May, 1919. The actions at Villers Cotterêts and Nery (to reach which place the

The forces in front of the First Army, now known to be British, had retired from about Compiègne and Noyon in the direction Senlis–Crépy-en-Valois–La Ferté Milon, and the western flank of the French presumably through Soissons in a southerly direction.

On the evening of the 1st September the Army was disposed as follows:

IV Reserve Corps about Quinquempoix;
II Corps south of Verberie to St. Sauveur;
IV Corps about Crépy-en-Valois;
III Corps Vauciennes-Villers Cotterêts;
IX Corps about Longpont, with its 17th Infantry Division at Champs.

The IV Reserve Corps in its march through Amiens had captured an enormous quantity of supplies, and in Noyon a vast amount of oats, straw, and hay was found.

In the meantime La Fère had been evacuated by the enemy, and the Second Army, after its rest day was over, advanced on the 1st September with its right wing to Brancourt and its cavalry to north of Soissons. On the 2nd September it was to continue the pursuit in a southerly direction, as the enemy had also retired on the front of the Third Army.

From a letter picked up on the evening of the 1st September it was found that it had been intended to give the British Army, 1st, 2nd, 3rd, and 5th Divisions, II Corps,[8] and 3rd and 5th Cavalry Brigades, a period of rest after midday the 1st September south of a line Verberie–Crépy-en-Valois–La Ferté Milon.

There thus appeared to be still a chance of reaching the enemy. The constant effort to give the troops of the First Army a rest day had to be again postponed in order to enable another enveloping attack to be made by the Army on the 2nd September. The Army Order issued at Noyon at 10.15 p.m. on the 1st September ran as follows:

German 4th Cavalry Division made a forced march of twenty-six hours) were the only serious attempts made by the Germans to interfere with the B.E.F. in the retreat after Le Cateau.
8. Thus in the original. The 3rd and 5th Divisions formed the II Corps.

'1. The enemy offered resistance today at Verberie–Crépy-en-Valois and at Villers Cotterêts. Farther to the south in the woods of Crépy and La Ferté Milon, as well as south of Verberie, the British had apparently three corps, besides cavalry.

'2. The I Cavalry Corps has advanced to the districts east of Soissons. The right wing of the Second Army advancing in a southerly direction will probably not go beyond Soissons tomorrow.

'3. The First Army will attack the British tomorrow –

'The II Corps west of the railway Orrouy–Nanteuil. Reconnaissances to be made east of the Creil-Paris road towards the east front of Paris;

'The IV and III Corps between the railway Orrouy–Nanteuil and the woods of Villers Cotterêts and the Ourcq. The line of demarcation between the two corps will be Vaumoise–Betz–Puisieux. The line Verberie–Villers Cotterêts will be crossed at 8 a.m.;

'The IX Corps, starting at 3 a.m., will advance east of the III Corps and of the woods of Villers Cotterêts in order to hold the enemy. Its 17th Division will move echeloned to the left. It will also cover the left flank of the Army and make reconnaissances to its left front, keeping touch with the I Cavalry Corps;

'The IV Reserve Corps, starting at 1 a.m., will reach Creil early in the morning. It will send out patrols west of the Creil–Paris road towards the north front of Paris;

'The Cavalry Corps will advance between the II and IV Corps and support the attack in co-operation with the left wing of the II Corps. It will send strong patrols to watch the north and north-east fronts of Paris as soon as possible;

'Army Headquarters will move at 11 a.m. from Noyon to Compiègne.'

These operation orders were, however, also fruitless, as the British Army escaped from the enveloping movement just in time and retired across the Marne to a line Meaux–La Ferté-sous-Jouarre and beyond towards Coulommiers. The II Corps came in contact with a French infantry and a British cavalry division about Ognon-Montepilloy, east of Senlis.[9] The

---

9. There were no British troops near Senlis. The retirement on the 2nd September was entirely unmolested by the Germans, in spite of Von Kluck's orders for attack, which only led to the German columns massing on their advanced guards.

enemy showed a strong opposition, but, with the assistance of the Cavalry Corps coming to the scene from Borest, he was defeated and pursued as far as Pontarme–Montaby.

A chance of dealing a decisive blow against the British Army was now no longer to be hoped for, and it was therefore decided to move the two corps on the left wing, the III and IX, in the general direction of Château Thierry against the flank of the French retreating from Braisne–Fismes on Château Thierry–Dormans in front of the Second Army.

In co-operation with the Second Army it might be possible to damage the French western flank very considerably. The First Army by its deep formation was in a position both to cover the flank and rear of such an attack and also to hold in check the garrison of Paris and the British.

Besides reports on the fighting east of Senlis the following also came in on the 2nd September: 'Strong enemy columns in retreat, about 11 a.m., from Braisne through Fère-en-Tardenois on Château Thierry and east of it. West of Fère-en-Tardenois large bivouacs still occupied at 11 a.m. South-west of Beauvais enemy seen retreating in direction of Gisors. East of Beauvais cavalry advancing towards Clermont. District west and north of Beauvais clear of the enemy.'

In the Army Orders issued at 1.15 p.m. and 2 p.m. from Compiègne the corps were kept well informed of the current events, and the latter Order stated that the Second Army was to cross the Aisne that day with its right flank moving through Soissons, and that the IX Corps would incline towards Château Thierry in order to take the retreating enemy in flank; the III Corps would also make for Château Thierry and advance as far as possible, sending on ahead cavalry with artillery, infantry on carts, and also machine guns, to support the IX Corps; it was also to reconnoitre the Marne as far as Vareddes. The IV Corps was to advance that day as far as the Therouanne stream about Oissery and Fosse Martin; the II Corps would continue its attacks east of Senlis and the IV Reserve Corps cut off the retreat of the enemy there to the west. Marwitz's Cavalry Corps was to remain on the right flank of the Army, and reconnoitre towards the north and north-east fronts of Paris, also towards the Marne up stream from Paris and along the right bank of the Oise towards Beauvais–Pontoise.

On the evening of the 2nd September the situation was appreciated at First Army Headquarters in Compiègne and resulted in the following Operation Orders being issued at 9.45 p.m.:

'1. Enemy columns are in retreat from the line Nanteuil–Dammartin as well as towards Meaux. The II Corps co-operating with Marwitz's Cavalry Corps has forced back the enemy at Senlis. There is no further information at hand as to the enemy south of the Marne, or on the line Meaux–La Ferté-sous-Jouarre.

'2. The Second Army today reached a line south of Soissons–Reims; tomorrow it will advance with its right flank moving from about Soissons towards Château Thierry.

'3. The IX Corps will continue its attack against the flank of the enemy retreating in front of the Second Army through Fère-en-Tardenois on Château Thierry. The III Corps will advance south of the IX Corps in the direction of Château Thierry. Cavalry and artillery, machine guns, and infantry on carts will be sent on ahead to attack the enemy when he crosses the Marne.

'4. The III and IX Corps will communicate with one another regarding the procedure of this attack. If contact is not obtained with the enemy both these corps will at once clear off to the westward off the road of advance of the right flank of the Second Army (VII Corps), from Soissons-Château Thierry. The III Corps will also reconnoitre towards the front La Ferté-sous-Jouarre–Château Thierry and report on the river crossings.

'5. The IV Corps will move tomorrow covering the right flank from Paris–Meaux to the vicinity of Crouy south of the road Betz–Mareuil–Brumetz. Reconnaissances to be made towards Meaux–La Ferté-sous-Jouarre. Corps Headquarters at Crouy.

'6. The II Corps will drive the enemy from the wooded country south of Senlis and march to about Nanteuil, keeping east of the Crépy-en-Valois–Nanteuil road. Corps Headquarters at Nanteuil. Reconnaissances to be made towards Dammartin–Meaux.

'7. Co-operating with the II Corps, the IV Reserve Corps will assist it to force back the enemy from the woods south of Senlis and will advance to the district east and north-east of Senlis, west of the billets of the Cavalry Corps. It will provide for its own security by a detachment at Creil and by outposts along the southern edge of the woods south of Chantilly and Senlis. Corps Headquarters at Rully. Reconnaissances to be made on the right flank beyond the Oise and towards the north front of Paris.

'8. Marwitz's Cavalry Corps is in billets west of the Crépy-en-Valois–Nanteuil road and will remain there tomorrow.

'9. Air reconnaissances will be made by the III, IV, and II Corps across the Marne in the directions allotted to the corps. The temporary bridges for heavy motor transport at Noyon and Compiègne are ready. The 18th Pioneer Regiment will follow the III Corps.

'Army Headquarters will move to La Ferté Milon tomorrow at 10 a.m.

'Special instructions have been issued regulating the communications behind the front and the movements of the Train and supply columns.'

The Intention of the Supreme Command to force the French South-eastwards from Paris

During the night of the 2nd/3rd September a wireless message arrived from the Supreme Command: 'The intention is to drive the French in a south-easterly direction from Paris. The First Army will follow in echelon behind the Second Army and will be responsible for the flank protection of the Armies.' The general directions of August 28th, which had ordered the First Army to move west of the Oise towards the lower Seine, had therefore been abandoned, and the wheel inwards of the First Army towards the Oise and its passage of the river about Compiègne and Noyon on the 31st August in order to exploit the success of the Second Army had evidently been approved by the Supreme Command. On the evening of the 2nd September, when that day's movements had been completed, the four corps of the First Army and the Cavalry Corps were still in the region of Creil–La Ferté Milon, north-east of Paris, ready for any operation west of the capital, against it, or east of it, whilst the IX Corps, like an arm of the Army reaching out to the left, was making the most creditable efforts to fulfil its mission and hold up the western flank of the retreating French Army by Château Thierry.

The First Army Commander considered that to force the enemy away from Paris in a south-easterly direction (which would involve the passage of the Marne and the Seine) would be a difficult and risky undertaking. There would probably be initial successes, but it would be scarcely possible in the circumstances to continue the offensive until the enemy was decisively defeated or partially annihilated. Another group of four or five divisions was needed by the Armies on the German right wing, in order effectively to guard the right flank against Paris and protect the long communications of the First and Second Armies, if the advance was to be continued into the centre of France. The Supreme Command, however, seemed to be firmly convinced that the garrison of Paris need not be taken into account for any operations outside the line of forts of the capital.[10] It is true that all the reports up to date seemed to confirm this point of view, but the situation of the flank armies might and would be most dangerous as soon as the French Higher Command was in a position to move a mass of troops from a part of the front where they could be spared through Paris, and thence begin a big offensive, making use of the great facilities for deployment from behind its extensive line of forts. The Supreme Command, however, had no anxieties with regard to the risks here suggested, and evidently placed complete confidence in the accuracy of its intelligence service on that point. At First Army Headquarters this view of the general situation also found many adherents. All the more urgently, therefore, did the First Army Commander renew his request for the long-delayed transfer to the front of the Brigade of the IV Reserve Corps retained by the Governor-General of Brussels, and for the relief by *Landsturm* and *Landwehr* troops of all the active units on the line of communications, so that they also might be brought up to the front. A further appreciation of the tasks of the First Army in these critical days was finally concentrated into a memorandum sent by the First Army Commander to the Supreme Command on the 4th September. This will be quoted later on.

On the 3rd September the IX and III Corps were ordered to move in accordance with the instructions contained in the first sentence of the above-mentioned wireless order of the Supreme Command. The IX Corps had crossed the Marne on the previous evening after heavy fighting at Chézy and Château Thierry, whilst its 17th Infantry Division had reached Oulchy-la-Ville. At this time the leading troops of the Army were on a line Pontarme–Montaby–Lagny-le-Sec–Fosse Martin–Rouvres, west of Mareuil–La Villeneuve-sous-Thury–La Ferté Milon–Troesnes.

The Second Army had crossed the Aisne with its right wing passing through Soissons, and was a good day's march behind the main body

---

10. The Supreme Command orders of the 2nd/3rd September quoted above ordered the First Army 'to follow in echelon behind the Second Army and to be responsible for the flank protection of the Armies.' These provided against attack from Paris direction. Von Kluck did not carry out these orders. His explanation for his disobedience follows below.

of the First Army. The Third Army was apparently to the left rear of the Second. Comparing this situation with the second sentence of the wireless order of the Supreme Command the conclusion was inevitable that if the First Army, now a day's march ahead of the Second, was to get in echelon behind it, it would then become impossible to force the enemy in a south-easterly direction, an operation which had been begun the previous evening by the 18th Infantry Division of the IX Corps by its occupation of the Marne crossings at and below Château Thierry. It fell to the First Army to apply the principal pressure in forcing back the enemy, as it was the only force that was immediately on his heels and that could exert the necessary compulsion on his line of retreat. On the other hand, if it halted for two days so as to get in echelon behind the Second Army, the enemy's Higher Command would regain the complete freedom of action of which it had been deprived. Should the First Army hold back, the great success for which the Supreme Command was confidently striving by 'forcing the enemy in a south-easterly direction' could no longer be hoped for. It was therefore fully in keeping with the spirit of the often-mentioned wireless order for the First Army to continue the pursuit as before across the Marne. The protection of the flank of the armies on the Paris side appeared to be provided for if the IV Reserve Corps with a cavalry division and the brigade expected from Brussels, together with the II Corps, halted echeloned towards the fortress capital, and if a thorough cavalry and air reconnaissance was insisted on. The IV Reserve Corps was to take up a preparatory position east of Senlis, the II Corps and the Cavalry Corps near Nanteuil-le-Haudouni. Army Headquarters were moved to La Ferté Milon behind the centre of the Army, which was now formed into two large groups each of three corps.

The last message of the Supreme Command, which, taken as a whole, required consideration of further points, led at the time to the following appreciation, which was Condénsed in the 'Memorandum' written in the spring of 1915, as follows:

'The First Army Commander had up till then – at La Ferté-Milon – imagined that the German plan of campaign had so far been carried out as arranged, that all the armies were advancing from victory to victory, and that the enemy was being decisively beaten along the whole front. That such was not the case – particularly that the German left wing to the south-west had withdrawn from the front of the French line of fortresses – was not realized at First Army Headquarters, owing to the scanty information which was given to it on the general situation of all the armies. The rapidity of the advance frequently made it difficult to maintain the telephonic cables leading to the rear, which were often destroyed by the inhabitants or by fire, sometimes accidentally by our own troops, and in other ways. Communication with the Supreme Command had therefore to be carried on mainly by wireless stations, which again were overworked in keeping touch with the Cavalry Corps and the neighbouring armies, a fact which the Army Commander was frequently made aware of by personal experience. There was consequently no means for the personal exchange of views so urgently needed between Army Headquarters and the General Staff of the Supreme Command. Nevertheless, no doubt existed at First Army Headquarters that the protection of the flank of the armies was increasing in importance as they advanced, and that the troops at the disposal of the First Army, which, under force of circumstances, had to be used for purposes of attack and flank protection simultaneously, would not suffice in the end for this. The reinforcement of the right wing by a group of about two corps appeared, therefore, to be absolutely indispensable.'

These reflections found expression in a wireless message sent to the Supreme Command on the morning of the 4th September, which ran as follows: 'The First Army requests to be informed of the situation of the other Armies, whose reports of decisive victories have so far been frequently followed by appeals for support. The First Army, which has been fighting and marching incessantly, has reached the limits of its endurance. It is through its efforts alone that the crossings of the Marne have been opened for the other Armies, and that the enemy has been compelled to continue his retreat. The IX Corps has won the greatest merit by its bold action in this respect. It is now hoped that every advantage will be taken of this success.

'The message of the Supreme Command No. 2220, in accordance with which the First Army was to follow in echelon behind the Second, could not be carried out under the circumstances. The intention to force the enemy away from Paris in a south-easterly direction was only practicable by advancing the First Army. The necessary flank protection weakens the offensive strength of the Army, and immediate reinforcements are therefore urgently needed. Owing to the ever-changing situation, it will not be possible for the commander of the First Army to make any further important decisions unless be is kept continuously informed of the situation of the other armies who are apparently not so far advanced. Communication with the Second Army is constantly maintained.'

On the evening of the 3rd September the following Operation Orders were issued to corps from La Ferté Milon:

'The leading division of the IX Corps has been in action on the high ground south-east of Château Thierry with the enemy retreating from Chézy on Montmirail. During the evening the enemy has extended his position through Courboin–Viffort towards Vieils Maisons. There are signs of the beginning of great disorder among the retreating columns. The enemy reported on the march today from Meaux to Coulommiers, apparently British troops, bivouacked this evening north of Coulommiers.[11] The area between Coulommiers and the neighbourhood of Vieils Maisons was reported by airmen to be free of the enemy. British cavalry was encountered this afternoon north of La Ferté-sous-Jouarre.[12] The Second Army has reached the Marne, with its right flank immediately east of Château Thierry. Tomorrow it is to advance with its right flank moving from Brasles through Confremaux and Corrobert, and the I Cavalry Corps from Château Thierry towards Montmirail.

'The First Army will continue its march across the Marne tomorrow, so as to force the French away eastwards. If the British offer opposition they are to be driven back.

'The IX Corps, co-operating with the VII Corps, will advance through Chézy-sur-Marne–Rozoy–Belleville, and along the road Château Thierry–Montmirail towards Montmirail.

'The III Corps will move through Bois Martin and Sablonnières towards St. Barthelemy, and by way of Vieils Maisons and Montolivet.

'The IV Corps will cross the Marne at La Ferté-sous-Jouarre and Saacy and advance in the general direction of Rebais.

'The II Corps, covering Paris, is to reach the Marne tomorrow west of La Ferté-sous-Jouarre, and send its advanced guards forward as far as the high-road Meaux–La Ferté-sous-Jouarre.

---

11. These were the 1st and 2nd Divisions. The others seem to have been well hidden.
12. This was the 5th Cavalry Brigade covering the retirement across the Marne.

'The IV Reserve Corps in conjunction with the II Corps will advance tomorrow to the vicinity of Nanteuil-le-Haudouin and east of it. It will be responsible for protecting the flank and the communications of the Army against Paris, and be ready to take part in the movements of the Army on the 5th September on the right flank. The brigade left behind in Brussels will probably arrive in Compiègne on the 5th September.

'Two divisions of the Cavalry Corps will march to La Ferté-sous-Jouarre. With regard to a later crossing of the Marne, it will communicate with the IV Corps, and, if necessary, with the III Corps. It will arrange with the II Corps for its march through the II Corps billeting area today. The Cavalry Corps will have one division opposite the north-eastern front of Paris: this division will remain tomorrow in its present billets, and will be under the orders of the general commanding the IV Reserve Corps.

'The demolition of the railways leading towards Paris from the north, north-west, and west is to be begun tomorrow. The Cavalry will also relieve the outposts of the IV Reserve Corps near Creil, and along the southern edge of the Forest of Senlis.

'The Marne bridges from Saacy to Château Thierry are in our possession, but there is no news to hand of those from La Ferté-sous-Jouarre westwards. The 18th Pioneer Regiment will follow the III Corps.'

Special instructions were issued for the lines of communication, and for the move of the advanced base to Chauny on the 5th September.

In conformity with the spirit of the often-quoted wireless order of the Supreme Command, the five corps of the Army were thus to make a long march in close formation south-eastwards, flank protection being carried out by the II Corps and the IV Reserve Corps, with the 4th Cavalry Division and the infantry brigade expected from Brussels on the 5th September.

On the 4th September the IV, III, and IX Corps reached the line Rebais–Montmirail, half-way between Le Petit and Le Grand Morin. The Cavalry Corps arrived at La Ferté-sous-Jouarre. The II Corps, as right flank corps of the Army, crossed the Marne and reached Trilport, east of Meaux.

Air reports stated that strong enemy forces were continuing the retreat southwards from the Coulommiers district, and also from about Montmirail, leaving rearguards to cover their movement. The

Second Army reached the line Pargny-la-Dhuis–Epernay, the Third Army reached Reims. On the evening of the 3rd September the Second Army had reported that 'the enemy in front is hastening back, utterly disorganized, to south of the Marne.'

The following Army Order, which is here given abridged, was issued from La Ferté Milon at 9.30 p.m., the 4th September, on the assumption that the Supreme Command still persisted in its resolution to force the enemy back from Paris in a south-easterly direction:

'The IX Corps advancing through Château Thierry attacked the enemy in flank on the 2nd and 3rd September, and brought him to a standstill. Today this Corps drove him back on Montmirail. Strong French columns are in retreat this evening from Montmirail through Esternay. The Second Army is to advance with its right flank from Pargny-la-Dhuis by way of Montmirail. Reims has been captured. The First Army will continue its advance tomorrow towards the Seine covering Paris. If the British can be reached in their retreat they are to be attacked. The corps are to move as follows:

'The IX Corps, after forcing the enemy back at Montmirail, will move with its right flank by Montenils–Le Vezier–Neuvy to about Esternay: it will avoid the Montmirail–Maclaunay–Sezanne road which belongs to the Second Army;

'The III Corps will advance with its right flank by St. Barthelemy and La Chapelle Verouge as far as Sancy;

'The IV Corps to the vicinity of Choisy reconnoitring towards Coulommiers–Rozoy as well as to its front;

'The II Corps will cross the Marne and advance to the lower reaches of the Grand Morin below Coulommiers, covering the flank of the Army from the eastern front of Paris;

'The IV Reserve Corps will advance tomorrow from about Nanteuil-le-Haudouin to the area Marcilly–Chambry, north of Meaux. It will be responsible for the protection of the Army north of the Marne from the north-eastern front of Paris;

'The 4th Cavalry Division on the right flank will remain under the orders of the IV Reserve Corps tomorrow. The remainder of the II Cavalry Corps will advance west of the IV Corps, and then in the direction of Provins. Its duty will probably be to attack the French flank while crossing the Seine;

'Army Headquarters will move tomorrow to Rebais.'

These movements were completed on the 5th September without difficulty.

Three corps, the IV, III, and IX Corps, with the II Cavalry Corps, formed the strong wing of attack to force the enemy in a south-easterly direction, and two corps, the II and IV Reserve, with the 4th Cavalry Division towards the south, constituted the covering flank against Paris. In addition the II Corps was in a position to attack the British, who were believed to be south of Coulomraiers and of the Grand Morin, should they make a stand there.

The conclusion of this advance marked the culminating point of the operations of the First Army, after an uninterrupted progress from the frontier of the Rhine Province to the far side of the Grand Morin and close to the middle reaches of the Seine.

Marches, whether of record length or short, had alternated with occasional local rest days and almost incessant fighting under conditions that did every possible credit to the mental capacity and physical endurance of the subordinate leaders and the gallant troops under their command.

The Army was unquestionably capable of carrying out further successful operations, but was not in a position to co-operate in extensive movements of the whole force demanding still greater efforts.

If the marches and battles of the corps and their transport columns and Trains are reviewed, it will be found that they establish a record of achievement which has seldom been obtained in the history of war. The season of the year favoured the campaign, epecially as regards the provision of an abundant and, for the most part, wholesome supply of food. The state of health of the troops was all that could be desired.

After the movements ordered for the 5th September had begun, a wireless arrived from the Supreme Command with fresh instructions. Sent off at 7 p.m. on the 4th September, it reached La Ferté Milon at 7.15 a.m. on the 5th, and read as follows: 'The First and Second Armies are to remain facing the eastern front of Paris: the First Army between the Oise and the Marne, occupying the Marne crossings west of Château Thierry; the Second Army between the Marne and the Seine, occupying the Seine crossings between Nogent and Mery inclusive. The Third Army will march towards Troyes and east of it.'

Whether and to what extent this decision of the Supreme Command had any connection with the report sent in by the First Army Commander on the 4th September was unknown at La Ferté Milon. It would, however, have been preferable if these orders had been sent out some days earlier. It was obvious that the offensive ordered to be made by the First Army to force the French away from Paris would not be in accord with the general situation, and would not have any chance of success unless the Central Intelligence Bureau had been able to ascertain, with the utmost certainty, that no considerable enemy forces were in a position to advance from Paris to attack the vulnerable flank and communications of the western wing of the German Armies. The situation was therefore appreciated, as follows, in La Ferté Milon: On the 3rd September the First Army had crossed the Marne with its advanced guards and today was approaching the Seine. To carry out the wireless orders of the Supreme Command would mean breaking away from the enemy, and making a two or three days' retreat. As regards the state of the enemy, First Army Headquarters had the impression that, although much exhausted by the fighting, in which he had suffered severely, he had none the less been able to retire in tolerable order. Should the pursuit be stopped, he would be able to halt and regain freedom of manoeuvre, as well as an offensive spirit. Taking this into consideration, it seemed preferable first to force him back over the Seine, and to postpone till then the wheeling of the First and Second Armies round to face the eastern front of Paris. Before the enemy forces now concentrating at Paris could be sufficiently strong and ready for battle, there would be time to finish the offensive against the Seine.

This appreciation was based on the assumption that, so far as was known at First Army Headquarters, the German Armies were advancing victoriously along the whole front, so that the enemy could not have any considerable forces available with which to threaten the German flank. To what extent this accorded with the actual situation could not be judged at First Army Headquarters, as was reported on the 4th September to the Supreme Command.

Accordingly, the suggestion set forth above was submitted both to the Supreme Command and to Second Army Headquarters; preparations, however, were made for carrying out next day, the 6th September, the wheel[13] ordered by the Supreme Command. The pursuit ordered for today, the 5th September, would be continued, since it had already started and fighting was in progress in places. The IV Reserve Corps and the Cavalry Corps would be halted, the latter on the Rozoy-Beton Bazoches road.

The IV Reserve Corps, on getting the order to halt at 10 a.m., had already reached its day's objective, its leading division, the 22nd Reserve Infantry Division, being in the area Marcilly–Chambry with the 4th Cavalry Division on its extreme northern flank. Air reports confirmed the fact that the enemy was continuing his retreat on the whole front from Paris to the Sézanne–Romilly road.

On the evening of the 5th September detailed instructions arrived from the Supreme Command, and from them it appeared that the enemy was transporting troops from the front Belfort–Toul westwards, and was also withdrawing troops from the front of our Third, Fourth, and Fifth Armies. The Supreme Command, therefore, calculated that very strong enemy forces were being concentrated near Paris to protect the capital and threaten the German right flank. The bearer of these instructions from the Supreme Command, Lieut.-Colonel Hentsch, gave a verbal account of the general situation, and, to the amazement of First Army Headquarters, who believed all the Armies to be advancing victoriously, it appeared that the left wing of the German Armies – namely, the Fifth, Sixth, and Seventh Armies – was held up in front of the French eastern fortresses, so much so that it could scarcely pin the enemy in front of it to his ground. There was consequently a possibility that the enemy would move troops by rail from his eastern wing towards Paris.

A very different aspect was thus given to the situation confronting the First Army. It was intensified by a report which arrived late in the evening of the presence of strong enemy forces about Dammartin, to the north-east of Paris.

Attack of the IV Reserve Corps towards Dammartin
Enemy forces had been already reported at, and south of, Dammartin on the 4th September to Headquarters of the IV Reserve Corps, which was

---

13. The movement ordered was hardly a wheel (*Schwenkung*).

responsible for the protection of the flank north of the Marne. When small detachments of the corps were sent out on the 5th towards St. Soupplets, and southwards to assist the 4th Cavalry Division to reconnoitre towards Paris, enemy columns were seen to be advancing from the district of St. Mard. The Corps Commander, General von Gronau, thereupon decided to attack, so as to clear up the situation more definitely about Dammartin, and, after a severe fight, the enemy was compelled to retire on the whole front of the corps – namely, from St. Soupplets to the high ground one and a half miles west of Penchard. The 4th Cavalry Division, advancing north of the IV Reserve, also came up against strong forces, whose attack it successfully repulsed, in the area Ognes–Bregy. The strength of the French was estimated at at least two and a half divisions, with a strong force of heavy artillery. In order that the advanced troops should not come within effective range of the Paris forts, and to avoid an envelopment of the right flank by the enemy forces in front of the 4th Cavalry Division, General von Gronau ordered that the pursuit was not to be continued beyond a line Cuisy–Iverny, and that as soon as it was dark a retreat would be made to behind the Therouane stream to a line La Ramé–Gué-à-Tresmes. This operation took place without any molestation by the enemy, who did not follow up at any part of the line.[14]

The first enemy attack against the imperilled flank of the First Army was thus repulsed, thanks to the brilliant leadership of General von Gronau, as also to the tenacity of his corps, and to the gallantry of the 4th Cavalry Division.

Concerning the Means of Communication with the Supreme Command, and their Instructions

As will have been already gathered from the foregoing account, the means of communication between the First Army and those in supreme command were totally inadequate. Some reasons for this have already been mentioned. Constant touch could be maintained with the Second

---

14. This is hardly correct. See 'Les Champs de l'Ourcq,' by J. Roussel-Lépine, where a vivid description of the following up of the German retirement by patrols is given, and, as Von Kluck himself states (p. 75), the French attacked the IV Reserve Corps again on the morning of the very next day.

Army, both at the front and between the two headquarters; but with the Supreme Command it was otherwise; through the breakdown of close communication, their orders to the rapidly moving First Army, which, during its wheel on the extreme flank of the Armies, had by far the greatest distance to cover, did not arrive till after the most important events had already begun. These orders will be more fully discussed later on from the point of view of First Army Headquarters.[15] For the lasting fame of the corps and their leaders, it must be mentioned here that the above-named bearer of the instructions of the 4th September from the Supreme Command expressed the general feeling of the Supreme Command that the achievements of the First Army had been beyond all praise. The Army was itself conscious of having fulfilled its duty up to the limit of what was humanly possible.

The Supreme Command instructions of the 28th August contained, as one of their most important items, the order that the First Army, with the Cavalry Corps, was to march west of the Oise towards the lower Seine. It was also to be prepared to co-operate in the fighting of the Second Army. Further, it was responsible for the flank protection of the Army, and had to prevent any fresh enemy concentrations in its zone of operations, which, broadly speaking, meant the area Compiègne–Abbeville–Dieppe–Rouen–Mantes–Creil. The Second Army, with the I Cavalry Corps, was to advance by La Fère and Laon on Paris. It had to capture Maubeuge and later La Fère, and then, in conjunction with the Third Army, to take Laon. These three Armies had to act in co-operation with one another, giving mutual support in the fighting in each other's sectors. Then followed the statement that the strong resistance which would be offered on the Aisne and later on the Marne might necessitate a wheel inwards of the Armies from a south-westerly to a southerly direction!

The First Army, as has been shown, at first continued its advance from the Somme in a south-westerly direction. According to the above instruction, the intention was to move the three Armies in a more westerly direction, so that the further advance of the First Army would have to be made west of the Oise towards the line Rouen–Mantes at a formidable

---

15. The German Supreme Command was at Luxemburg at this period of the campaign, and until after the Battle of the Marne.

part of the Seine. Its immediate objective would be to destroy any enemy forces in that neighbourhood, and, if possible, to drive them into the Seine and occupy the Seine crossings. It was an attractive objective, but not to be attained, since, the strength of the western wing Armies being what it was, an advance in the direction Beauvais–Vernon could only be made subject to the possibility that part, if not the whole, of the First Army might at any moment have to be wheeled inwards in an easterly direction, to support the neighbouring Armies. The inadequate strength of the western wing of the German Armies, which stood in need of transference of large forces from the eastern wing, was a decisive obstacle to any extensive operations of this nature. A rumour, current at First Army Headquarters, that it might be intended that the Army should later come in behind the French and British Armies by advancing across the line Lower Seine–Dreux–Etampes, was set aside as baseless, in view of the hopeless inadequacy for such a purpose of the forces of the German western wing. Besides, troops would have to be retained for a position of observation north-east to north-west, covering Paris, and an endless line of communications would have to be guarded.

Towards the end of August and beginning of September the First Army Commander had considered that a restraining influence might have been exercised with advantage by the Supreme Command, with a view to a more coherent strategy. A pause in the operations would give time for a rest, time for the arrival of several divisions from Lorraine, time for the occupation of the Marne district, and time for a real investment of Paris from the right banks of the Seine and the Marne, including an artillery bombardment of the north-eastern front of Paris with all the heavy artillery of the First Army, and as much of that of the Second Army as could be got up. As soon as the Armies had reorganized and recuperated, and strong forces arrived from Lorraine, and when all active units on the lines of communication had been relieved by *Landwehr* and *Landsturm* troops, and the brigade from Brussels was back with its corps, then a war of movement could reasonably be begun again. The enemy, of course, would likewise be able to recover again and bring up reinforcements, and also gain a greater freedom of manoeuvre, but this would appear to be the lesser evil – unquestionably so as soon as a sufficient force had been transferred to the German right flank as suggested above. The despatch of reinforcements to the German Army in the East at the expense of the Western Armies, as happened in August, would be avoided until the French Army had been decisively beaten. After that, a provisional release of part of the Armies in France would be begun, and full attention could be given to reinforcing the Army in Eastern Germany. Much might occur in the political world. President Poincaré's Government, for instance, which had been hastily removed to Bordeaux on the appearance of the German right wing in front of Paris, might manifest inclinations towards peace.

Whether, however, a checking of the advance of the German right wing would be considered necessary by the Supreme Command depended entirely on the general situation as a whole. If French forces were being transferred on a large scale behind the front, and an attack against the flank of the First Army was at all probable, a halt was essential. The whole plan of campaign, which depended on rapid execution for its success, would thereby break down. The First Army Commander was quite unaware of the all-important fact that the Fourth, Sixth, and Seventh Armies were being held up east of the Moselle, and thus allowing the enemy there freedom of manoeuvre. Had this been known in time, the idea of crossing the Marne with any large forces of the First Army would not have been entertained!

On the 29th August the First Army had begun the wheel from a south-westerly direction towards the Oise, and desired to advance through Compiègne and Noyon on the 31st, so as to follow up the successful Battle of St. Quentin reported by the Second Army.[16] The Supreme Command agreed to this decision.

The wireless order of the 28th August to march west of the Oise towards the lower Seine was consequently set aside for the moment. Perhaps the deciding factor against it was the belief that, should the offensive be continued on a very broad front, the western wing was not sufficiently strong to crush the French left wing, the British Army, and a possible sortie by the Paris garrison, and at the same time to invest the great fortress-capital. The protection of the flank from Lille to Rouen against the Channel coast had also to be taken into consideration.[17]

---

16. Von Bülow, in his book 'Mein Bericht zur Marneschlacht,' claims to have suggested this move.
17. The value of sea power is evident here. There were fourteen Territorial divisions in being.

In the Higher Commands there was thus no such under-estimation of the enemy as was met with in less responsible or wholly irresponsible quarters. Nevertheless, there seemed every probability that, during September, further disabling defeats could be inflicted on the enemy by a timely massing of superior forces in the zone of the three right-wing Armies, and either breaking through the front or enveloping the flanks, or both.

During the night of the 3rd September the third wireless order from the Supreme Command arrived, and at a most decisive moment. The French were to be forced back in a south-easterly direction from Paris; the First Army was to follow in echelon behind the Second Army, and would henceforth be responsible for the flank protection of the Armies.[18] On these orders the movements were begun which were fundamentally altered on the evening of the 4th September by an order for the Armies of Kluck and Bülow to close round the north and east front of Paris from the Oise to the Seine, which apparently was the result of the wireless report from First Army Headquarters sent on the morning of the 4th September.

The difficult backwards wheel of the Army was now to commence that led to the bloody battle on the Ourcq, and brought the First Army to Nanteuil-le-Haudouin and Baron, in its effort to force Maunoury back against the Therouane and on Hammartin, and disorganize his Army.

---

18. As it had been throughout.

Chapter 4

The Battle on the Ourcq

The Crisis and the Break-away – The March Back to the Aisne
Before describing the important events that occurred during the
second week in September with the help of Army Orders and of the
Memorandum of 1915, and showing what calls were made on the moral
strength and manoeuvring capacity of the corps of the First Army and its
Cavalry Corps, it seems an appropriate moment to discuss the enemy's
appreciation of the general situation.

According to Major Gedel's book,[1] 'The Origin of the World War and
its Progress on the Belgian–North French Theatre till Mid-September,
1914,' as well as other authorities, it appears that on the 4th September
General Gallieni, as Governor of Paris, ordered the French Sixth Army
of General Maunoury, which was under his orders, to hold itself in
readiness to march from its billeting area between the northern front of
Paris and the advanced position of Dammartin, which was a strong one,
and (apparently) fortified with heavy artillery.[2] Early on the morning of
the 5th September, Maunoury was to attack the flank of the German First
Army. The Commander-in-Chief, Marshal Joffre, had received a wireless
report of Gallieni's decision on the morning of the 4th September, and
he thereupon issued the following Operation[3] Orders on the evening of
the 4th:

'1. Every advantage is to be taken of the dangerous situation of the
German First Army by a combined movement of all forces of the Allied

---

1. This is the French book mentioned in the opening pages.
2. This was not the case.
3. *Author's Note.* – This is an extract and not authenticated. (The orders agree
   generally with the version given by M. Babin in his 'La Bataille de la Marne'
   and other French authors.)

Armies on the extreme left (French) wing. All preparations will be made on the 5th to begin an offensive on the 6th.

'2. The general position to be occupied by the evening of the 5th is as follows:

'(a) All the available strength of the Sixth Army will be in a position of readiness in the north-eastern zone of Paris, so as to be able to cross the Ourcq between Lizy and May-en-Multien in the general direction of Château Thierry; the available forces of General Sordêt's cavalry will be under the orders of General Maunoury to assist this movement. The opponent will be Von Kluck.[4]

'(b) The British Army is on a line Mangis–Coulommiers ready to attack facing east in the general direction Montmirail. The opponent will be Von Kluck.

'(c) The Fifth Army will extend slightly to its left and take up a general line Courtacon–Esternay–Sézanne, ready to attack in a general direction south to north; the II Cavalry Corps (General Conneau) will be responsible for maintaining touch with the British Army. The opponents here will be Von Kluck and Von Bülow.

'(d) The Ninth Army (General Foch) will cover the right flank of the Fifth Army; it will hold the southern exits of the marshes of St. Gond, and part of it will deploy into the plain north of Sézanne. The opponents will be Von Bulow and Von Hausen.[5]

'3. The offensive will be commenced by the various Armies on the morning of the 6th September.'

Similarly the Fourth Army (De Langle), on the right of the Ninth[6] Army, was to attack in a northerly direction: opponent, Duke Albrecht of Würtemburg. The Third Army, Sarrail, was to deploy in a westerly direction against the left flank of the Crown Prince.

The underlying idea of preparing to close round the German Western Armies, like Hannibal at Cannae, was clearly in the minds of the French General Staff. Although the initial suggestion to this end, and the decision to envelop the German western wing, may have come from General

---

4. This last phrase does not occur in the published French versions.

5. This last phrase does not appear in the published French versions.

6. *Fifth* in the original, which is obviously erroneous.

Gallieni, it was converted into a double envelopment by Joffre and his Staff.

Though the enemy must be given full credit for the idea, the result of it cannot have come up to his expectations. Hannibal in his wonderfully planned battle mastered the fortune of war, whereas it eluded Joffre, confronted as he was by leaders who grasped the situation – and reversed it. To be named in the same breath as the Punic general is, however, an honourable recognition for leaders of our times on whichever side they stood in this titanic struggle. Tannenberg is another example, and similarly Mukden (see Oscar Wiedebautt's 'Hannibal bei Cannae')[7]

According to Major Gedel the French Sixth Army, after a long and exhausting march on the 2nd September, had assembled north of Paris as follows: north of Dammartin, General Lamaze with the 55th and 56th Reserve Divisions, and a Moroccan Brigade; at Louvres, between Dammartin and St. Denis, General Vautier with the 14th Division of the VII Corps and the 63rd Reserve Division; and north of Clayes, Gillet's Cavalry Brigade. The 61st and 62nd Reserve Divisions under General Ebner reached Pontoise on the 4th September in a very exhausted condition, and were to move to Attainville on the 6th. The 45th Algerian Division (General Drude) marched on the evening of the 5th from Bourg-la-Reine to Dammartin as the General Reserve of the Army. Finally, the IV Corps under General Boelle was being detrained from the 3rd to the 7th September at Gagny, south of Le Raincy. Taken all round there were ten infantry divisions and the cavalry of General Sordêt and General Gillet, including the eight or nine battalions of Zouaves and Spahis, which were to arrive on the 9th. Forming the permanent garrison of Paris were the 83rd, 85th, 89th, and 92nd Territorial Divisions and the Marine Brigade of Vice-Admiral Ronarich.

And yet the assembly of such a mass of troops on the flank of the German western wing had been kept secret.[8]

Plutarch, in his 'Maxims of Kings and Commanders,' says that Chabrias the Athenian named as the greatest commander he who knows

---

7. A magazine article on Cannae by the late Chief of the German General Staff, Von Schlieffen, has led to this battle being quoted by nearly every recent German writer on war.

8. Even by Von Kluck's dating, which is approximately correct, they came up gradually and were rushed on to the battlefield. They were never 'assembled.'

best what is going on behind the enemy's lines. The vital importance of the intelligence service in modern war was brought out on this occasion in a most vivid manner.[9]

The Right-Flank March of the First Army

The Army Order quoted below and issued at 11 p.m. on the 5th September from headquarters at Rebais, behind the front of the, until now, offensive wing of the First Army, was based on the belief that there was as yet no great danger threatening the right flank, and that a march back to cover it could be carried out without interruption. In any case, some big move would have to be made without delay to meet the situation. The Order ran as follows:

'1. When the First Army, in conjunction with the Second Army, has forced back the British and French opposed to it to the Seine, both Armies are ordered by the Supreme Command to remain facing the eastern front of Paris, and to act offensively against any enemy operations from Paris: the First Army between the Oise and the Marne, the Second Army between the Marne and the Seine. Air reports state that strong enemy forces are in retreat on Tournan and Rozoy, as well as from Courtacon towards Provins, and from Esternay towards Nognet-sur-Seine.

'2. The First Army, in order to fulfil this fresh task, will begin its march to face right as follows:

'The II Corps will march in two columns by Trilport to Germigny, and by Pierre Levée and Monteaux to Isles-les-Meldeuses; it will send back its transport via La Ferté-sous-Jouarre along the road Vendrest–Crouy.

'The IV Corps will reach the vicinity of Doue tomorrow; and its transport will remain where it is.

'The III Corps will go to the vicinity La Ferté Gaucher tomorrow. Its transport, in two echelons, will move to Charly-sur-Marne along the north bank of the Marne, and to the neighbourhood Lizy–Clignon, respectively.

---

9. The complete failure of the German Intelligence Department, under Major Nikolai, has been frequently referred to in the German press (*vide* H. Binder's 'Was wir als Kriegsberichterstatter nicht sagen dürften'), but Von Kluck might at least have kept in touch with the 61st and 62nd Reserve Divisions who retired before his left flank.

'The IX Corps will remain in its billeting area tomorrow, and move its transport via Nogent to the northern bank of the Marne. The transport will be parked east of the road Coupru–Domptin–Charly-sur-Marne;

'The II and IV Corps will leave weak rearguards behind on the Grand Morin.

'3. The movements of the transport columns and trains will be regulated daily by Army Headquarters until further orders. As soon as the Army has completed its change of position, fresh instructions will be issued for the communications with the advanced base at Chauny.

4. Corps Headquarters will arrange for Staff Officers to superintend the orderly crossing of the Marne by the transport columns and train.

'5. The Marne bridges are to be strongly occupied at once: by the II Corps at Lizy and Germigny; by the IV Corps at La Ferté-sous-Jouarre–Saacy and Nanteuil, including the railway bridge; by the III Corps at Charly-sur-Marne and Nogent; and by the IX Corps at Chézy-sur-Marne and Château Thierry, including the railway bridge.

'6. The II Cavalry Corps will screen the right-flank march of the Army from the south-east [*sic*] of Paris, and the lower Seine by making a demonstration towards Lumigny and Rozoy.

'7. The 18th Pioneer Regiment will march on La Ferté; it will be attached to the IV Corps for administrative purposes.

'8. Army Headquarters will be at Charly-sur-Marne from 10 a.m. onwards. Orders will be issued at 6 p.m. The 2nd Battalion of the 24th Regiment, with a machine-gun section, will be sent there to guard Army Headquarters.'

The application of Caesar's maxim, that 'in great and dangerous operations one must act, not think,' necessarily produced in this critical situation rapid alterations in the movements of the First Army. One kept in mind also how the mighty genius of the Great and Unique Frederick displayed itself, in situations strategically speaking hopeless, in a lightning succession of victories, with all their political consequences.

During the night of the 5th September it became obvious that further and more drastic changes in the movements of the First Army were essential, if the danger of an envelopment was to be effectively countered in time. Owing to the reports of the IV Reserve Corps in its fighting during the 5th, a special order was sent to the II Corps to begin its march in the early hours of the 6th, so as to be ready to support the IV Reserve

Corps on the 6th if needed. Its commander, General von Linsingen, moved the 4th Infantry Division by Lizy towards Trocy and the 3rd by Vareddes, to the relief of the IV Reserve Corps, which in the meantime had been attacked by about a corps of the enemy on the front Bregy–St. Soupplets–Penchard. The 3rd Infantry Division came up against strong British forces west and north of Vareddes.[10] The first strong reinforcement to deal with the new opponent had thus arrived on the scenes.

By an Order issued at 5.30 p.m. the IV Corps was withdrawn across the Marne to the district north of La Ferté-sous-Jouarre, so that in case of necessity it could be put into the fight, the enemy having now brought superior forces into action. At 10.30 p.m. the IV Corps was ordered to move again that same night, so that at dawn it would be in a position to attack across a line Rozoy-en-Multien–Trocy. Thus, on the morning of the 7th September, the II Corps, the IV Reserve Corps (still without its Brussels Brigade), and the IV Corps stood between the Therouane and the Gergogne (a tributary of the Ourcq), with their units rather intermingled, with the 4th Cavalry Division immediately to the north of them: they were to hold up the Army of Maunoury, of the strength and composition of which nothing was known at First Army Headquarters. The pressure of superior forces was perceptible from the very first.[11]

The situation on the front of the III and IX Corps on the evening of the 6th was as follows.[12] The enemy had attacked during the morning from west of the Forest of Traconne in the direction Escardes-Seu, where the

---

10. There were no English forces within ten miles of Vareddes, nor did any of them come in contact with the II Corps on the 6th. The Moroccan Brigade is probably meant.

11. Von Kluck's own account of Maunoury's Army, taken from Major Gedel's book, quoted on p. 89, disproves that it was on the 6th/7th September superior in force to his troops.

12. Von Kluck's memory appears to fail him here. According to Von Bülow ('Mein Bericht zur Marneschlacht'), Von Kluck handed him over command of the III and IX Corps on the evening of the 6th, but at 11.15 a.m. on the 7th sent a message: 'Assistance of III and IX Corps on Ourcq is urgently required; enemy considerably reinforced. Send Corps in direction La Ferté Milon and Crouy.' This message is clear evidence that Von Bülow's statement is correct.

IX Corps stood ready about Esternay. In spite of having already begun the withdrawal as ordered, the corps decided to make a counter-attack in order to facilitate the progress of the Second Army fighting on the Petit Morin. The III Corps had also begun its withdrawal, but, in view of heavy artillery fire which opened in front of it, together with a request for assistance from the IX Corps, it decided to hold itself in readiness in the area Saacy–Montceau, to support the IX Corps. By an Order of the 6th September issued at 5.25 p.m., the III Corps was to take over the protection of the right flank of the IX Corps.

The Second Army, wheeling round, pivoted on its right flank at Montmirail, intended to continue the pursuit up to the Seine with its centre and left wing, the latter moving on Marigny-le-Grand. The III and IX Corps thus came in front of the right wing of the Second Army.[13] By an Army Order issued at 10 p.m. that evening both these corps were therefore withdrawn to the line Sablonnières–Montmirail on the northern bank of the Petit Morin. They gained touch again with the right flank of the Second Army at Montmirail, and, to ensure united action, were to conform to its instructions.[14] Marwitz's Cavalry, which had advanced to Lumigny and Rozoy, covered the right flank of the III Corps against the enemy forces advancing from about Tournan towards Coulommiers. It gave up the 2nd Cavalry Division to the I Cavalry Corps, which had been sent forward by the Second Army Commander into the Montmirail district.

The French Attack
According to a report from the Supreme Command, General Joffre had ordered the general attack of the French Armies for the 7th September in order to bring about the decisive battle.[15] If this was true, the fate of the

---

13. Von Bülow, in his book already quoted, complains bitterly that the First Army, instead of being 'echeloned behind the Second Army,' as ordered, was 'echeloned in front of it – its left Corps (IX) pushed itself completely in front of the right Corps (VII) of the Second Army.'
14. Von Bülow, as above quoted, says they were placed under his orders when Von Kluck went north on the 6th (see note, p. 92).
15. It is stated by various German writers that a copy of General Joffre's orders was captured.

French offensive, in the opinion of the First Army Commander, would depend on the strength and success of the attack delivered from Paris against the flank of the German Armies. In order not merely to repulse the enemy in that quarter, but to defeat him by an outflanking counter-attack from the north, the IX and III Corps were ordered to march early on the morning of the 7th September in the direction La Ferté Milon-Crouy, and their relations to the Second Army as regards instructions given them by it were cancelled.[16]

The critical nature of the situation demanded this step, for First Army Headquarters believed that the Second Army, in the course of the wheel it intended to make in accordance with Supreme Command orders issued at 7 p.m. on the 4th September, would advance south of the Marne in a westerly direction. As a matter of fact, however, it came up against strong resistance and did not get beyond the Petit Morin.

The Lines of Communication Headquarters were ordered to send forward all available troops from the advanced base at Chauny to Villers Cotterêts to reinforce the attacking wing of the First Army. Referring again to the Army Orders of the 6th September, issued at 10 p.m. and at 10.30 p.m. from Rebais, the IX Corps had to move all its transport and Train on to the Nogent-l'Artaud–Château Thierry road north of the Marne, and beyond again towards Rocourt St. Martin on the road to Soissons; the III Corps was to move its transport and Train on to the Charly–Lizy–Clignon road. The zone of march of the III and IX Corps hurrying northwards was to be absolutely cleared. At 7 a.m. on the 7th September First Army Headquarters moved from Charly-sur-Marne to Vendrest, near the II, IV, and IV Reserve Corps, which were fighting west of the lower Ourcq.

In the second Operation Order issued on the evening of the 6th the II Corps was directed to move all its transport and train on to the Coulommiers–Chézy-en-Orxois–Noroy road and to cross to the north of the Coulombs-Crouy road by 1 a.m. that night. The country in the rear of the Army was thus clear.

---

16. As stated in the footnote, p. 92, Von Kluck sent a message to Von Bulow asking for them to be sent to him, and thus exposed the right flank of the Second Army.

About midday on the 7th September the corps on the Ourcq came into action under the general command of General von Linsingen, commanding the II Corps, as follows: the northern group, consisting of the 7th Infantry Division and the 4th and 16th Infantry Brigades, under General Sixt von Armin, commanding the IV Corps, on the line Antilly–Acy-en-Multien; the centre group, consisting of 8th Infantry Division (less the 16th Infantry Brigade) and the 7th Reserve Division, under General von Gronau, commanding the IV Reserve Corps, on the line Vincy–Manceuvre, immediately north-west of Trocy; the southern group, consisting of the 22nd Reserve Division and the 3rd Infantry Division, under General von Trossel, on the line Trocy–Vareddes.

This formation of groups had become unavoidable because, owing to the increasing gravity of the situation, the divisions had to be thrown into the fighting singly as they became available, and they thus became separated from their own corps. It was practically retained till the Army arrived on the Aisne in order to prevent the crossing and congestion of columns adding to the difficulties of the withdrawal.

At 12.15 p.m. General von Linsingen ordered an attack across a line Antilly–Acy–Trocy. This offensive was planned as a wheel pivoting on the left flank, against which the weight of the enemy's attack was being directed, and which was suffering heavily from the enfilade fire of hostile artillery. The attack of Linsingen's group made good progress; its right wing drove the enemy back through Villers St. Genest and Le Bas Bouillancy, and the 22nd Reserve Division took and held Etrepilly. A considerable part of the offensive wheel had been carried out, though a decision was by no means arrived at.

In order to give as much support as possible to the left wing, which was being severely cut up by the enemy's artillery fire from about Meaux, the following Operation Order was issued from Vendrest at 1.15 p.m.:

'The IV Reserve and II Corps are heavily engaged on a line Betz–Vareddes, north of Meaux. The enemy has been reinforced north of Meaux and our left wing taken in enfilade by heavy artillery fire from that direction.

'The III and IX Corps will press forward immediately as far as possible to support it, and the eastern wing of the Army[17] must come into action by tomorrow morning at the latest.

---

17. That is, the III and IX Corps, which had been left behind with Von Bülow.

'The westernmost division of the III Corps will march by the shortest route to Lizy. One infantry brigade of this division, with the heavy artillery of the III Corps, as well as some cavalry, will march along the La Ferté-sous-Jouarre road towards Trilport. The bridges at Ussy and St. Jean, west of La Ferté-sous-Jouarre, have been destroyed. This brigade with enfilade gun fire should silence[18] the British artillery.

'Reconnaissances will be made and protective measures taken towards Coulommiers, where the enemy is reported, and also towards the lower Grand Morin. Communication will be kept up with the II Cavalry Corps, which, with artillery, will operate today from about Trilport. The other three divisions will march under the orders of General von Lochow by the shortest route towards La Ferté Milon–Crouy.'

At 2.30 p.m. another Army Operation Order was issued, which, together with the facts published in the 2.15 p.m. Order, shows up the crisis in a clearer light:

'General of Infantry von Linsingen will continue in command of the II, IV, and IV Reserve Corps today according to the former group-formation of commands. The following units are marching up to his support:

'1. The 2nd Battalion of the 24th Regiment, less one company, with a machine-gun section and two guns from Charly to Lizy, which has been guarding Army Headquarters will arrive this evening and await instructions at Lizy.[19]

' 2. The II Cavalry Corps will come into action from Trilport today, its guns enfilading the enemy artillery north of Meaux.

'3. The III and IX Corps are on the march from the south-east towards La Ferté Milon–Crouy. One division of the III Corps is sending an infantry brigade and the corps heavy artillery to Trilport to take in enfilade the British artillery north of Meaux.[20] The main body of the division is on its way to Lizy.

---

18. The original German *Soll* seems to convey doubt that this object will be attained.
19. The situation must have been considered very serious for the Headquarters Guard to be sent into the fight.
20. There was no British artillery north of Meaux. Again, the Moroccan Brigade was where Von Kluck located British.

'I wish to express my warmest praise to the Generals and the troops under their command for their splendid achievements.

'(*Signed*) Von Kluck.'

Anxiety as regards a sweeping victory still weighed upon the Army Commander and his Chief of the Staff, who was constantly examining the situation from all points of view. The wheel back of the First Army had already accomplished much.

On the 7th the 6th Infantry Division reached Charly-sur-Marne and the IX Corps was back on the Marne close to Chézy. Army Headquarters remained at Vendrest, where they were able best to communicate with all parts of the battle-front. The country north of Crépy-en-Valois as far as La Ferté Milon was reported clear of the enemy, as also Senlis, Creil, and Verberie; on the other hand, strong forces were about Nanteuil-le-Haudouin on the evening of the 7th.

To enable the reader to follow the onward rush of coming events in their main outlines from the standpoint of the First Army Commander, and also the supplementary measures called for by the increased urgency of the situation, it seems preferable to go on giving all the chief Army Orders, either verbatim or in excerpts, even at the cost of some repetition, when describing events so important.

At 9.15 p.m. on the 7th September the situation as it appeared to First Army Headquarters in Vendrest is shown by the following Army Order for the 8th:

'The II, IV, and IV Reserve Corps have maintained their positions today on the line Antilly-Puisieux-Vareddes. Strong enemy forces bivouacked this evening at Monteuil [*sic*], Silly-le-Long, St. Soupplets and west of it. Fresh enemy forces came into action this afternoon at Betz. Weaker forces are opposed to us along the lower Grand Morin, and about a division south of Coulommiers.[21]

'The Second Army is engaged on the line Montmirail-Fere Champenoise.

---

21. Von Kluck failed to discover that the British Expeditionary Force was working eastwards on the 7th.

'The II, IV, and IV Reserve Corps will remain in group formation as before under the command of General von Linsingen. The enemy has fought the battle mainly with his strong force of heavy artillery on his right southern wing and in the centre.

'It will be necessary to hold the positions gained and entrench there. The left wing at Vareddes will have to bend back during the night into a more favourable position. On the right wing the offensive will be pressed forward on the arrival of reinforcements.

'The III Corps will start at 2 a.m. from Montreuil and La Ferté-sous-Jouarre and march by Mareuil and Crouy so as to come into action on the right flank of the group under General Sixt von Armin, north of Antilly. It is desirable that artillery with cavalry should be sent on ahead.

'The IX Corps will start at 2 a.m. from the south of Château Thierry and march north of the II Corps on La Ferté Milon.

'The II Cavalry Corps (less the 4th Cavalry Division) will cover the left flank of the Army towards the lower Grand Morin and Coulommiers; it will also operate from about north of Trilport against the enemy's artillery in position north of Meaux.

'Army Headquarters are to remain at Vendrest.

'A battalion of the infantry brigade of the IV Reserve Corps marching from Brussels and a battalion of the 2nd Grenadier Regiment arrived this evening at Villers Cotterêts and are attached to the group under General Sixt von Armin.'

At 9.15 a.m. on the 8th September another Army Order seemed necessary, by which the 5th Infantry Division was sent through Cocherel towards Trocy in order to stop an attempt of the enemy to break through at that part of the line. Further, the left column of the IX Corps was ordered towards Mareuil and its right column towards La Ferté Milon.

The enemy was reported to be advancing from about Coulommiers and south of it towards La Ferté Gaucher and Rebais. The Guard Cavalry Division was in a covering position on the Petit Morin facing Sablonnières, and the 2nd Cavalry Division at La Ferté-sous-Jouarre.

One regiment of infantry and a brigade (three batteries) of artillery was to be detailed from the left column of the IX Corps to be ready at Montreuil-aux-Lions, eight miles north of La Ferté-sous-Jouarre, as a reserve at the disposal of the Army Commander. The line of communication for transport columns was Château Thierry–Epieds–Fère-en-Tardenois–Fismes.

The Order concluded by pointing out that the deciding factor of the day lay in the arrival into action of the IX Corps on the front La Ferté Milon-Mareuil. 'The corps must under no circumstances be deterred from coming into action on this front by any advance of the enemy on Coulommiers.'

It is convenient here to anticipate a little, and to mention that on the evening of the 8th the 6th Infantry Division came into action in support on the right flank of the Army at Cuvergnon, north of Antilly, and that the IX Corps was in a position of readiness that evening to envelop the enemy's northern wing on the 9th by attacking from the line La Ferté Milon–Mareuil on the right and to the north of the 6th Infantry Division. Although the enemy had sent forward reserves from Nanteuil-le-Haudouin to the Bois du Roi, an envelopment of his northern flank seemed assured, especially as Von Lepel's 43rd Reserve Brigade of the IV Reserve Corps had reached Verberie on the 8th from Brussels via Compiègne; it was to march on the 9th through Baron and take the enemy in rear. On the 8th, the 10th *Landwehr* Brigade (Colonel von Lenthe), marching behind it, reached Ribecourt.

General von Lochow was to take over the command of the centre group, consisting of the IV Reserve Corps and the 8th Infantry Division, on this day.

With the flank of the Army on the Marne and its front west of the Ourcq an effective envelopment of the enemy's northern wing seemed certain.

The British Advance

During the morning of the 8th September it became evident that the British were advancing towards the Marne, while strong forces were marching north of the Grand Morin on La Ferté-sous-Jouarre–St. Cyr and by Kebais on Orly. The security of the flank and rear of the Army did not yet seem sufficiently provided for by the II Cavalry Corps along the Marne west of La Ferté-sous-Jouarre, and by the I Cavalry Corps on the Petit Morin between La Ferté and Villeneuve. An order was therefore sent to the IX Corps at 11.20 a.m. to occupy the line of the Marne from La Ferté-sous-Jouarre to Nogent-l'Artaud, so as to guard it against this flanking movement of the British, but in the end only an infantry brigade and two field artillery regiments[22] were sent, and the General Reserve at Montreuil-aux-Lions was handed over to the Corps Commander. The Marne bridges were to be prepared for destruction, and, if necessary, to be demolished; in the latter case, the fact was to be notified to headquarters.

Meanwhile, the French attempt to break through our front at Trocy on the morning of the 8th had been frustrated without the assistance of the 5th Infantry Division, which was ready at hand in support. Late in the evening, Army Headquarters went to La Ferté Milon in order to be close to the critical part of the battle. At dusk an audacious detachment of French cavalry[23] had attacked an aeroplane station south of La Ferté Milon, just as the line of cars of Army Headquarters was approaching the scene of the action. All the members of the Staff seized rifles, carbines, and revolvers, so as to ward off a possible advance of the French cavalrymen, and extended out and lay down, forming a long firing-line. The dusky red and clouded evening sky shed a weird light on this quaint little fighting force. The thunder of the artillery of the IX and IV Corps boomed and roared defiantly, and the gigantic flashes of the heavy guns lit up the deep shadows of the approaching night. In the meantime, the French squadrons had been apparently shot down, dispersed, or captured by troops of the IX or another Corps.[24] These bold horsemen had missed a goodly prize!

The Army Operation Order for the 9th September, issued from La Ferté Milon late in the evening of the 8th, stated that the First Army had maintained its position on the whole front from Cuvergnon, north of Betz-Antilly, to the Marne salient at Congis; also that enemy reserves were

---

22. Six batteries each. A composite brigade ('Brigade Kraewel') of six battalions, six batteries, and a machine-gun company, was formed to reinforce the cavalry. (See *Militär Wochenblatt*, 8th December, 1919.) It is mentioned below in the text without explanation.

23. This was Gironde's squadron of the 22nd Dragoons in the raid of the 5th Cavalry Division led by General Cornulier-Lucinière. (See 'Le Rôle de la Cavalerie Française à l'aile gauche de la première bataille de la Marne,' by J. Héthay.)

24. There was only one squadron. It lost 2 officers and 25 men *vide* Héthay, quoted above).

reported south and west of Crépy-en-Valois. A decision would be arrived at on the morrow by the enveloping attack of General von Quast with the IX Corps and the 6th Infantry and 4th Cavalry Divisions from the wooded country north of Cuvergnon. The Infantry Brigade of Von Lepel was to press forward from Verberie towards Baron, west of Nanteuil-le-Haudouin, and the group of General Sixt von Armin – the 16th Infantry Brigade, and the 7th and 4th Infantry Divisions – would, if he thought fit, co-operate by taking the offensive. The strength of this wing of attack was therefore five and a half infantry divisions and the 4th Cavalry Division, in addition to Lepel's Infantry Brigade.

By the same Army Operation Order, the left wing, under General von Linsingen, was ordered to maintain its position, and General von der Marwitz was to protect the left flank of the Army on the Marne with his 29th Cavalry Division[25] and Von Kraewel's Composite Brigade from Montreuil-aux-Lions.

Army Headquarters would move to Mareuil at 9 a.m. on the 9th, to which place telephonic communication would be established.

The IX Corps had already received special instructions from Vendrest giving the general situation as mentioned above, and stating the Army Commander's intention that all the available leading troops of the Corps should, if possible, come into action on that day, the 8th, to assist the 6th Infantry Division, on the flank of which Colonel von der Schulenburg had already arrived with two battalions. The remainder of the IX Corps was to be brought forward, so that it might come into action early on the 9th, as stated above.

The Gap in the Western Wing of the German Armies

At 9.30 a.m. on the 9th September Army Headquarters arrived at Mareuil. Early in the morning General von Quast had advanced with his IX Corps, the 6th Infantry Division, some *Landwehr* battalions under Von der Schulenburg, and the 4th Cavalry Division, to make the enveloping attack towards Nanteuil-le-Haudouin. His right wing moved south of Crépy-en-Valois, through the Bois du Roi. Up till 2 p.m. the attack was still making good progress, and the enemy did not seem to have any more

---

25. 2nd and 9th Cavalry Divisions must be meant.

strong reserves at his disposal. Lepel's Brigade had reached Baron, on the Senlis–Nanteuil-le-Haudouin road, before meeting any opposition, and our indefatigable airmen reported that the roads in the area Senlis–Chantilly–Creil–Compiègne were clear of the enemy.

While the progress on the wing of attack was thus all that could be desired, important developments on the left wing of the Army, which was seriously threatened, called for further action by the Army Commander. The Second Army had had to withdraw its right wing on the 8th on Fontenelle, near the source of the Dollau [? Dollan], and at 7.35 a.m. on the 9th reported that it was withdrawing its right wing on that day to the line Margny–Le Thoult. The I Cavalry Corps, pressed by the enemy, was retiring partly on Condé-en-Brie and partly across the Marne. A report from General von der Marwitz, despatched at 10.20 a.m. and received at 11 a.m., stated that a strong force of British infantry was advancing across the Marne at Nanteuil and Charly.[26] Under these circumstances, the left wing of the Army under General von Linsingen was ordered at 11 a.m. to be sent back to a line Crouy–Coulombs, left of the lower Ourcq; and the 5th Infantry Division, which had not yet been put into the battle, was to march from Trocy towards Dhuisy to attack the British forces crossing the Marne. By an order issued at 12.35 p.m. this division was placed under the orders of General von der Marwitz, who was guarding the left flank of the Army at La Ferté-sous-Jouarre, and with Kraewel's Brigade north-east of that place.[27] At 10.30 a.m. he had sent in a report, received at 12.42 p.m., that the British forces on this side of the river were being attacked, which was entirely in accordance with the wishes of the Army Commander.

The wing of attack was still advancing between La Ferté Milon and Crépy-en-Valois. From a telephone conversation with the Chief of the Staff of the II Corps it appeared that, owing to the state of the battle on the Ourcq, it was not yet necessary to withdraw the left wing of the Army.

---

26. The whole British Expeditionary Force was crossing – 1st Cavalry Brigade, followed by the 1st and 2nd Divisions at Charly; the 3rd and 5th Divisions at Nanteuil and Saacy, 4th Division at La Ferté-sous-Jouarre and east of it.

27. Thus the British were opposed by the 5th Division, Kraewel's Composite Brigade, I Cavalry Corps (two divisions), and II Cavalry Corps (two divisions only, as 4th was on Von Kluck's right).

With the consent of Army Headquarters, the group under General von Linsingen therefore remained in its former position.

Shortly after 1 p.m. the following wireless message arrived from the Second Army: 'Airmen report the advance of four long enemy columns towards the Marne; at 9 a.m. their advanced troops were on the line Nanteuil–Citry–Pavant–Nogent-l'Attaud. The Second Army is beginning to retreat, its right flank on Damery.' This retreat widened the gap between the two Armies, which up till now had been screened, into a serious breach in the western wing of the German Armies, extending – with every possibility of a further increase – from Château Thierry to about Epernay – that is to say, on the breadth of front of an Army. Not till twenty hours later did the Second Army Headquarters correct their message by another to say their right flank was retiring not on Damery, but on Dormans.[28]

The attack of General von der Marwitz against the British ended successfully, and part of the enemy who had crossed the Marne was thrown back into the vicinity of Montbertoin by evening.[29]

Towards midday the situation of the First Army was thoroughly favourable, even taking into consideration the withdrawal of the Second Army north-eastwards. For victory seemed assured on the decisive wing of attack, the left wing was standing firm, and the flank appeared to be sufficiently guarded by General von der Marwitz with two cavalry divisions, the 5th Infantry Division, and Kraewel's Brigade. At about this period Lieut.-Colonel Hentsch, on the Staff of the Supreme Command, arrived at Mareuil from Second Army Headquarters. His arrival was only made known to the Army Commander after he had already hastily departed – a regrettable circumstance, which would have been avoided had the Colonel personally reported himself to the Army Commander; the latter at the moment was close to the scene of the meeting.[30]

---

28. Damery is ten miles east of Dormans. The mistake made the gap forty miles instead of thirty.
29. Monbertoin on French maps. It is a collection of houses just south of Montreuil-aux-Lions. The British 14th Infantry Brigade was delayed there by Kraewel's Brigade, but was not thrown back.
30. It would appear to be the fault of Von Kluck's Chief of Staff that Colonel Hentsch did not see him. Hentsch, of course, as is the service custom,

Colonel Hentsch made the following communication, which was taken down in the form of a minute in the still existing records of First Army Headquarters:

'The situation is not favourable. The Fifth Army is held up in front of Verdun and the Sixth and Seventh in front of Nancy-Epinal. The retreat of the Second Army behind the Marne is unalterable: its right wing, the VII Corps, is being forced back and not voluntarily retiring. In consequence of these facts, all the Armies are to be moved back: the Third Army to north-east of Chalons, and the Fourth and Fifth Army, in conjunction, through the neighbourhood of Clermont-en-Argonne towards Verdun. The First Army must therefore also retire in the direction Soissons–Fère-en-Tardenois, and in extreme circumstances perhaps farther, even to Laon–La Fère. (Lieut.-Colonel Hentsch drew the approximate line to be reached by the First Army with a bit of charcoal on the map of Generalmajor von Kuhl, Chief of the Staff.) A new Army was being assembled near St. Quentin, so that a fresh operation might be begun. General von Kuhl remarked that the attack of the First Army was in full swing and that a retreat would be a very delicate operation, especially as the Army was in an extremely exhausted condition and its units intermingled. To this Lieut.-Colonel Hentsch replied that there was nothing else to be done; he admitted that, as the fighting stood at the moment, it would not be convenient to retire in the direction ordered and better to go straight back to behind the Aisne with the left flank at least on Soissons. He emphasized the fact that these directions were to remain valid regardless of any other communications that might arrive and that he had full powers.'

It must be repeated that information of such a kind, throwing an entirely different light on the whole situation, should have been given by Lieut.-Colonel Hentsch direct to the Commander of the First Army.

The Withdrawal to the Aisne

From French sources now available, it is clear that General Maunoury had so early as the evening of the 8th considered the advisability of a retreat

---

would report first to the General Staff. The Supreme Command showed its opinion of Von Kluck shortly after, on 10th September, by putting him under Von Bülow again.

to a position of defence on the line Monthyon–St. Soupplets–Le Plessis Belleville. A tactical victory of the First Army over the Army of Maunoury on the extreme left wing of the French forces seemed indeed certain, and it was possible that by the continuation of the offensive on the 9th a far-reaching success might have been obtained. It is probable also that the British could not have come forward very rapidly at first after the fight at Montbertom.[31] Nevertheless, after the instructions from the Supreme Command, there could be no longer any doubt as to the necessity for the retreat ordered. To what extent any further considerable successes of the First Army might influence the course of the operations of the German Armies fighting to the east of it was, from the standpoint of the First Army Commander, a question not to be ignored. In the opinion of the Staff Officer from the Supreme Command provided with full powers such, however, was not the case. The breach between the two Armies on the right wing threatened to open still wider, thus uncovering the flank and rear of the First Army, whilst the Second Army would naturally improve its situation as it continued its withdrawal in a north-easterly direction. The full advantages of the success already begun against Maunoury could be reaped with certainty within the next few days; but the breaking away from the enemy and the reorganization of units which would then be necessary, as well as the bringing up of fresh supplies of ammunition and food, moving forward the trains and making the communications secure – all being measures requiring time to carry out – would enable the British force only temporarily held up at Montbertoin and other British columns immediately east of it, as well as the left wing of the more mobile Army of General d'Esperey, to come up on the flank and in rear of the First Army, which had already reached the limits of its powers of endurance. Unless it is assumed that the enemy would make extraordinary mistakes, the First Army would then have to isolate itself from the other Armies by a withdrawal in a northwesterly direction towards Dieppe, or in more favourable circumstances towards Amiens – in any case, a long march, with a corresponding wastage of man-power. It would have been a very different matter had the group of two or three corps from Lorraine

31. The British Expeditionary Force advanced ten to fifteen miles on the 10th against opposition, so the supposed German success at Monbertoin does not seem to have affected it (see p. 103, footnote).

or Alsace, so long desired, been ready at hand to support the offensive of the western wing Armies, or fill up the gaps. After following up to a certain extent its victory against Maunoury, the First Army might then have withdrawn through Clermont and Compiègne by short and comfortable marches, protected by strong rearguards with heavy artillery, and have reorganized in a suitable position on a new front, preparatory to starting another offensive above or below Soissons in conjunction with the newly assembled Army.

In view of the completely altered situation, the Army Commander, fully conscious of the tremendous consequences of his decision, decided to begin the withdrawal immediately in a northerly direction towards the lower Aisne, between Soissons and Compiègne. Once the decision was made, the situation called for its execution without delay. Not a single hour was to be lost. Army Operation Orders were issued from Headquarters at Mareuil at 2 p.m. and at 8.15 p.m., as follows:

'The situation of the Second Army has necessitated its withdrawal behind the Marne on both sides of Epernay. By order of the Supreme Command, the First Army is to be withdrawn in the general direction of Soissons, to cover the flank of the Armies. A new German Army is being assembled at St. Quentin. The movement of the First Army will begin today. The left wing of the Army, under General von Linsingen, including the group under General von Lochow, will therefore be first withdrawn behind the line Montigny–Brumetz. The group under General Sixt von Armin will conform to this movement so far as the tactical situation will allow, and take up a new line from Antilly to Mareuil. The offensive of the group under General von Quast will not be proceeded with any further than is required for the purpose of breaking away from the enemy, so that it will be possible to conform to the movement of the other Armies.

'(*Signed*) Von Kluck.'

The Army Operation Order issued in the evening for the 10th September ran as follows:

'The right wing of the Army was today advancing victoriously towards Nanteuil-le-Haudouin. On the left wing, the 5th Infantry Division with the II Cavalry Corps attacked the enemy advancing on the front Nanteuil-sur-Marne–Nogent-l'Artaud. By order of the Supreme Command, the First Army is to be withdrawn towards Soissons and west of it behind the Aisne, so as to cover the flank of the Armies; the Second Army is in retreat to behind the Marne on both sides of Epernay.

'I wish to express to the men of the First Army my highest admiration for their devotion to duty, and for their exceptional achievements during this offensive.

'The Army will today continue the movement ordered, from the lines already reached, the main body moving up to and north of a line Gondreville-south-east of Crépy-en-Valois–La Ferté Milon–upper half of the Ourcq line. The left wing of the Army under General von Linsingen, including the group under General von Lochow, will march east of the Ourcq, below La Ferté Milon, and then, with its right flank along the road La Ferté Milon–Villers Cotterêts–cross-roads four and a half miles north-east of Villers Cotterêts–Ambleny. General Sixt von Armin's group will march with its right flank on the Antilly–Vauciennes–Taillefontaine–Attichy road. General von Quast's group will keep to the west of it.

'The II Cavalry Corps, with Kraewel's Brigade, will cover the left flank of the withdrawal. The 4th Cavalry Division has been ordered to move ahead to the Aisne to occupy the bridges between Compiègne and Soissons. The Reserve Brigade of Von Lepel and the composite 11th *Landwehr* Brigade of Von der Schulenburg will march by Compiègne to Vic for the same purpose. In addition to the rearguards holding up the enemy, his advance will be further obstructed by breaking up the roads and demolishing the bridges over the upper Ourcq. The 18th Pioneer Regiment will be sent forward by the column it is now with, to the Aisne, and if possible, its transport will accompany it. Preliminary measures for reorganizing corps units will take place to morrow.

'Army Headquarters will move today to La Ferté Milon. Orders will be issued there at 7 a.m. tomorrow morning.

'(*Signed*) Von Kluck.'

Thus, on the evening of the 9th, the Army Commander was able to watch the columns of his whole Army on the march again, and on the 10th the reshuffling of the smaller units began, after which it was hoped that same day to start re-forming the larger units.

The enemy at first did not follow up at all, and later only with hesitation; it was conjectured that this was owing to the exhausted state of Maunoury's Army, the confusion among its units, and his expectation of unpleasant surprises. That this estimation of the condition of the French Sixth Army was correct is shown by an official account of the battle given to representatives of the Press by the French General Staff later on, which may be appropriately quoted here. According to the version of it given in the *Kolönische Zeitung* of the 6th December, 1914, No. 1323, it was as follows:

'By the evening of the 8th it was obvious that our movement eastwards had failed. Instead of outflanking the German right wing, Maunoury had to be careful lest he himself was enveloped. To escape this fate, he ordered all the troops of the IV Corps still available to be sent on to his left flank at Nanteuil-le-Haudouin; these troops were sent up by rail and by motor-cars, whilst some were sent in motor-buses requisitioned from Paris, or else by march-route. By the time they arrived, however, the situation had become much worse: German troops were reported on the Nanteuil–Senlis road as far as Baron, thus threatening the retreat on Paris. Late on the afternoon of the 9th our IV Corps had to retire from about Nanteuil, and one wondered what the situation might be by the following morning. The Sixth Army Commander, however, begged his commanders to stand at all costs, in order not to lose the fruits of the victory on the Marne.'

It can be seen from this how seriously the success of the First Army on the Ourcq was regarded by French Headquarters, and, further, that a German Reserve formation of four to six divisions must have brought about the destruction of the French left wing and thereby could have transformed the whole general situation of the right wing of the German Armies.[32]

The Order of the Day, issued by General Maunoury[33] after the five days' battle on the Ourcq, strangely contradicts in places the above account of the situation of his Army; it runs as follows:

---

32. A similar reinforcement of General Maunoury, or of Field-Marshal French, would have been equally fruitful in results.

33. This is authentic.

'For five complete days the Sixth Army has fought without cessation or rest against a numerous enemy, whose fighting spirit had been raised to an exceptional pitch by his former successes. The fight was a severe one; and the heavy losses incurred, the great exertions needed, and the lack of rest and even food surpass all description. You have, however, borne them all with a fortitude, constancy, and endurance which no words of mine can adequately praise. Comrades, your commander asked you to do more than your duty for the sake of your country. You have fulfilled it beyond all possible limits, and, thanks to your courage, victory crowns our colours. Now that you have gained this glorious reward, hold on to it. If I have helped to it in any way, I feel myself rewarded by the greatest honour that has fallen to me in a long career – namely, to have led such heroes as you. It is with deep emotion that I offer you my thanks for your achievements, for in so doing I thank you for that to which all my energies and strength have been devoted for forty-four years – revenge for 1870. Thank you, and all honour to the men of the Sixth Army.'

Barais Deltour, at the conclusion of a treatise on the Battle of the Marne, writes: 'No one dared to utter the word Victory, and it was only invented months afterwards for the Battle of the Marne.'[34]

---

34. This treatise has not been identified, and, in any case, the author's name bears no weight, and he is wrong. On the 9th September, 1914, itself, the victory was recognized, as is proved by the Order of the Day issued to the French Fifth Army by General Franchet d'Esperey on that day from his Headquarters at Mont-mirail. It contains the words 'victors' and 'victories,' and this summary of the situation, which explains why victory was claimed: 'Held on both his flanks, his centre broken, the enemy is now retreating towards east and north by forced marches.'

The British Official 'Eyewitness,' writing on the 14th September, uses these words: 'It was only on this day (11th September) that the full extent of the *victory* gained by the Allies on the 8th was appreciated by them '("Eyewitness's' Narrative of the War,' pp. 7 and 15). Some German regiments fled, leaving their colours behind. In one field there were hundreds of German lances abandoned by German cavalry in their headlong flight. Von Kluck himself has quoted at the end of a paragraph (four above this) in a translation of a French document, issued in Germany early in December. 1914 (which must, therefore, have appeared in France, if it is genuine, some time earlier), the phrase 'the victory of the Marne.'

During the 10th September the withdrawal of the Army came to a standstill with the main body of the marching columns in the area north of the wooded country about Villers Cotterêts, whilst their rear-guards halted south of the woods on an approximate line east of Crépy-en-Valois–Grumilly, north of the upper Ourcq. The plunge of the great columns of the Army into the forest zone must have made it difficult for the enemy to discover their whereabouts. Marwitz's Cavalry Corps, with Kraewel's Brigade, covered the left flank of the Army, and by the evening was in the vicinity of the upper Crise near Soissons; whilst Lepel's Reserve Brigade and Schulenburg's *Landwehr* Brigade protected the right flank about Compiègne, and the 4th Cavalry Division was occupying the bridges over the Aisne between Attichy and Soissons, as ordered. The Army Commander went to Coeuvres-et-Valsery, whither the Chiefs of Staff of all the Corps were summoned to discuss the measures required to get corps units in their right places again, to arrange lateral troop-movements, the withdrawal of trains across and beyond the Aisne, and to regulate the further details of the food and ammunition supply, and the question of billeting areas.

The retreat was carried out, for the most part, without any friction. The great strain which had naturally been put on the columns and trains made an occasional stimulus necessary to hurry them along. The enemy did not pursue in the true sense of the word: he had clearly expected the battle to be continued on the 9th and 10th September, and therefore found himself behind time as soon as the new operation began. The only exception to this was that rearguard fighting with a strong force of enemy's cavalry, probably British, took place on the front of Marwitz's Cavalry Corps,[35] and the other troops under his command, because movement on the roads to be used by them was particularly cramped by the baggage columns and train moving ahead of them; however, here, too, the break-away from the enemy was accomplished without serious damage.

On the evening of the 10th September the Army Commander described the situation between the upper Ourcq–Aisne and Oise–Marne, and

---

35. The British cavalry cut off and captured a number of German rear parties on the 9th; on the 10th, owing to the ground being soaked by rain, the action between the two cavalries was entirely by gunfire. French cavalry divisions captured a long column of waggons belonging to Von der Marwitz's Corps.

explained the further duties in front of the Army in the following Army Operation Order issued from Coeuvres-et-Valsery at 10.30 p.m.

This order marks an all-round slackening of the pressure on the First Army as right flank guard of the German forces, and it indicates that, though the group arrangements still subsisted, the first steps were being taken to get the divisions back again to their proper corps, while the transport columns and trains were being moved up on to the high ground north of the Aisne arranged in their original formations, so as to clear the river-crossings for the fighting troops: it runs as follows:

'1. Air-reports state that during the afternoon the enemy has been in pursuit with strong forces of all arms on Neuilly St. Front and Chézy-en-Orxois. Smaller columns were also seen about Coulombs, Vendrest, and Ocquerre. A strong force of enemy's cavalry with considerable artillery has been in action about Billy, and later, farther to the north-east, with part of the left wing of the Army and the Cavalry Corps. There are no air-reports at hand yet from the country west of the lower Ourcq. A French Brigade of cuirassiers with artillery appeared on the western wing of the Army. Lepel's Reserve Brigade had to retire yesterday on Verberie, after a victorious action in the vicinity of Rully against superior numbers. The Second Army is retiring behind the Vesle on both sides of Reims.

'2. Tomorrow the First Army will cross the Aisne at Soissons and west of it, leaving strong rearguards on the southern bank, and will begin the reorganization of its units.

'3. Starting at 5 a.m. the 7th and the 22nd Reserve Divisions will cross the Aisne at Fontenoy and Pommiers in front of the left wing of the Army, under General von Linsingen. The IV Reserve Corps will then assemble south of Nouvron. Leaving their billets at 5 a.m., the following units will take up entrenched rearguard positions: the 5th Infantry Division with Kraewel's Brigade, and the heavy howitzer battalion of the III Corps, between Belleu and Billy; the 3rd Infantry Division between Saconin-et-Breuil and the Crise; the 8th Infantry Division from north-east of Laversine to Saconin-et-Breuil.

'4. Of the group under General Sixt von Armin, the 7th Infantry Division will take up a rearguard position to the west of Laversine in touch with the 8th Infantry Division. Starting at 5 a.m., the 4th Infantry Division will move from Vivières through Ressous-le-Long and Fontenoy to the neighbourhood of Pasly, and rest there.

'5. Of the group under General von Quast, the 6th Infantry Division, marching at 5 a.m., will move through Attichy–Bitry–Riviere–Tartiers–Chavigny–Cuffies to Crouy, north-east of Soissons. It will halt and rest about Tartiers till the country east of that village is clear of transport columns and trains. One division of the IX Corps will cross the Aisne at Berneuil and remain there; its other division will move at first to about Guise Lamotte.

'6. The Cavalry Corps will cover the left flank of the Army about Acy and Serches, and prevent any attempt by the enemy's cavalry to pass round by Soissons against the rear and communications of the Army. The 4th Cavalry Division will secure the right flank of the Army beyond the IX Corps by the Forest of Compiègne.

'7. Army Headquarters will move to Fontenoy tomorrow: orders will be issued at 6 p.m.

'8. The movements of the transport columns and trains will be regulated tomorrow by Colonel von Berendt, who will receive special instructions from Army Headquarters. All commanders of ammunition columns and train units will report at 6 a.m. tomorrow morning to Colonel von Berendt at the exit from Soissons towards Coucy-le-Château.

'9. At the conclusion of tomorrow's movements the Corps Commanders will take over their commands.'

The lack of disorder and friction during the retreat, and the regrouping of divisions and other units into their right places, was due to the untiring energies of the Chief of the Army Staff and the Chiefs of the Corps Staffs.

Before Army Headquarters left La Ferté Milon, the Army Commander had sent to His Majesty the Emperor a report on the successful battle of the First Army on the Ourcq, also on the preliminary operations before breaking away from the enemy, the withdrawal to the Aisne, and the measures taken for covering the right flank of the Second Army by the First. In the meantime, early in the morning of the 10th September a wireless message from the Supreme Command, despatched at 2.30 a.m., arrived:

'Second Army has retired to behind the Marne, right flank Dormans. First Army will place itself in echelon behind it in a position of readiness. Envelopment of the right flank of the Second Army is to be prevented by offensive measures.'

At about 9 a.m. this order was supplemented by another: 'Fighting on the whole front favourable. Security of right flank of Second Army by an offensive of First Army urgently needed.' After the arrival of Army Headquarters at Coeuvres-et-Valsery, information was received that the First Army would be under the orders of the Second Army Commander till further notice. In view of these orders the Second Army Commander at 3.35 p.m. asked when the First Army would be ready to take the offensive again. As will have been seen, however, from the Army Operation Order issued from Coeuvres-et-Valsery, another offensive at this moment was out of the question. The Army Commander therefore decided to bring every unit of the Army on to the northern bank of the Aisne before anything else, and not to begin preparations for another offensive until this had been done and till after the corps had finished their reorganization and the most necessary fighting supplies had been replenished. The First Army would not be ready for employment in any other way before the 12th September at the earliest.

On the evening of the 10th (Second) Army Headquarters communicated that the Second Army was to be withdrawn behind the Aisne by the 12th with its left wing at Thuizy south-east of Reims, the Third Army to the line Mourmelon-le-Petit–Francheville, and the Fourth Army to behind the Rhine–Marne Canal as far as Revigny.

Crossing the Aisne

On the 11th September the movements ordered for crossing the Aisne and re-forming the corps were completed without any appreciable disturbance by the enemy. That evening a division of the IX Corps stood north of the Aisne at Berneuil; the IV Reserve Corps, less the Brigade of Von Lepel, was at Nouvron; the 4th Infantry Division about Pasly, north-west of Soissons, and the 6th Infantry Division at Tartiers, east of Nouvron. South of the Aisne, the other half of the IX Corps, the IV Corps, and the 3rd and 5th Infantry Divisions held entrenched positions on a line Cuise Lamotte–Laversine–Saconin-et-Breuil–Billy. Passing through the position of the IV Corps, the Army Commander was able to convince himself that its battle-formation, as always, was eminently suited to the situation; and later, in the Aisne valley at Pommiers, he watched the 22nd Reserve Division crossing the river below Soissons in the most excellent order. There was no sign of uneasiness or anxiety, and everywhere the same keen, enterprising spirit in spite of the need for a rest.

Army Headquarters went to Fontenoy. The protection of both flanks of the Army lay in safe hands. The withdrawal of the trains proceeded well according to orders. The enemy's advanced guards did not come up against our strong front till the evening. Artillery fire without any serious fighting followed.

On the morning of the 11th September the following Order arrived from the Second Army Commander: 'The Second Army is to reach the Vesle on both sides of Reims by the 12th September. The First Army will continue its withdrawal to behind the Aisne on the 11th, and on the 12th and 13th will close in, covered by the Aisne position, up to the right flank of the Second Army. From the morning of the 11th the Vesle at Braisne and Fismes will be held by a composite brigade, detailed from the Second Army.'[36]

According to a later message the right flank of the Second Army was to go to Chalons-sur-Vesle. The 13th Infantry Division was to remain at Braisne and Fismes, with the I Cavalry Corps farther to the south. The enemy was following the right wing of the Second Army, and had reached Ville-en-Tardenois. As regards the Seventh Army,[37] information came from its commander to the effect that the XV Corps was on its way by rail to St. Quentin, and the last of its fighting troops might be expected to arrive by the 13th September. Had this happened ten days earlier at Soissons, the fortunes of the campaign would have turned very materially in favour of the German right-wing Armies, and transformed the general situation.

The First Army in Position North of the Aisne
The Army Operation Order issued from Fontenoy at 8 p.m. on the 11th September informed the Army that the enemy's advanced guards had appeared on the front, that Compiègne had been bombarded by a detachment of Maunoury's Army, that the 13th Infantry Division had

---

36. At this time Von Kluck's left was at Soissons, ten miles as the crow flies from Braisne.
37. This was in process of formation to fill the gap between the First and Second Armies, and eventually comprised the XV Corps and VII and IX Reserve Corps.

arrived on the front Braisne–Fismes, and that the Second Army was along the Vesle on both sides of Reims. It then ran as follows:

'3. The First Army will take up a position of readiness north of the Aisne tomorrow.

'4. Starting at 2 a.m., those units of the Army still south of the Aisne will move across to the northern bank, masking their withdrawal by rearguards. The divisions already on the northern bank will take up positions to cover the retirement: all heavy artillery to be on the northern bank. The positions of the IV Corps will be taken over by the IV Reserve Corps on the high ground at Nouvron and Vaux: they will be occupied at daybreak. All train and baggage south of the Aisne are to be sent on immediately by the roads mentioned in paragraph 5.

'5. The roads are allotted as follows: the 5th Infantry Division of the III Corps with Kraewel's Brigade of the IX Corps by Venizel to the high ground about Condé. The 6th Infantry Division from Tartiers through Bieuxy–Bagneux–Juvigny–Terny Sorny to Nanteuil-la-Fosse. The 3rd Infantry Division of the II Corps through Soissons on to the high ground about Crouy and Bucy-le-Long. Soissons is to be strongly held. The road through Vaux is allotted to the IV Corps. The 4th Infantry Division will take up a position of readiness on the ground about Pasly. The 8th Infantry Division of the IV Corps will move through Pernant and through Mercin-et-Vaux to Pommiers, where there are two bridges, and thence to north of Juvigny. The 7th Infantry Division will march through Ambleny and Fontenoy to the area south of Tartiers. The 17th Infantry Division of the IX Corps will go into position along the high ground from Attichy to Bitry; the 18th will march through Attichy and Vic to Autreches and north of it. Lepel's Reserve Brigade will move from Compiègne to Nampcel.

'6. General von der Marwitz with the 2nd and 9th Cavalry Divisions will be responsible for protecting the left flank of the Army as before, and will get into touch with the Brigade of the VII Corps at Braisne. The 4th Cavalry Division, supported by the IX Corps, will guard the right flank of the Army.

'7. The Aisne bridges allotted to corps are to be prepared for demolition by them and held after they have been crossed: if the enemy presses forward they are to be destroyed. The temporary bridges are to be dismantled after the crossing has been completed.

'Army Headquarters will be at Juvigny; the 6th Infantry Division will detail a company as guard. Orders will be issued at 6 p.m. I myself shall be at Nouvron from 6.30 a.m. onwards.

'(*Signed*) Von Kluck.'

With the conclusion of these movements the Army, within the three days 9th–12th September, in three large strides had regained touch with the Second Army, at the same time breaking off the battle, reorganizing its units, and moving away to the north-west. The gap between the two Armies was closed, though only by a thin line of troops.

Mention must also be made of the movements of the transport, including all the trains, ammunition, and baggage columns, which, during its withdrawal from the Grand Morin to the Ailette, clearly showed that by war experience it had grown to its work, and had accomplished a difficult task, demanding great physical and moral effort, in a praiseworthy and devoted manner. Of the transport of the III Corps, the first line marched from Terny Sorny through Margival to Chavignon, the second line from Leuilly through Vauxaillon and Anicy-le-Château to Chaillevois; of the II Corps the first line transport marched from Juvigny through Leuilly to Vauxaillon, second line from Crécy-au-Mont through Landricourt to Brancourt. The second line transport of the III Corps had to be clear of Leuilly by 10 a.m., and the first line of the II Corps was not to reach Leuilly before 10.30 a.m.; of the IV Corps the first line transport marched from Vezaponin to Crécy-au-Mont, the second line from Troisly Loire to Coucy-le-Château, and remained halted; and of the IX Corps the first line marched from Nampcel to Audignicourt, and the second line from Blerancourt to Saint-Paul-aux-Bois.

The general movement in a north-easterly direction applied equally to the transport as to the fighting troops, so that both drew closer to the Second Army in their withdrawal.

The Attack by the Armies of Maunoury and French across the Aisne

On the morning of the 12th September strong columns were reported advancing northwards from the neighbourhood of Hartennes and

Fère-en-Tardenois on the upper Ourcq, which were clearly the British, who could only move slowly in large bodies. Weaker forces of Maunoury's Army were reported to be advancing in a northerly direction about Mortefontaine and Cceuvres-et-Valsery, and from the Villers Cotterêts district. The area Roye–Montdidier–Noyon on the right flank of the Army and west of the Oise was clear of the enemy.

During the afternoon the enemy approached the Aisne, and by that time strong gun fire had developed on the whole front of the Army, especially opposite the IX Corps. A serious attack by the enemy was all the more probable since it was of great importance, from the point of view of General Maunoury and General French, to defeat the First Army before German reinforcements could arrive. At 1 p.m. the following Operation Order was issued: 'The Army will maintain its positions. The IX Corps has been directed to cover the right flank of the Army on the front Nampcel–Audignicourt–Autreches. The distribution of front line sectors is as follows:

'IV Reserve Corps on the high ground at Nouvron.'
'IV Corps on the high ground at Cuisy-en-Almont to the heights of Pasly (both inclusive).
'II Corps from Cuffies to about Chivres.'
III Corps on the high ground north of Condé, with one division in reserve.
'Marwitz's Cavalry Corps at Vailly.'

The positions were strong, the right flank was safely protected and the left flank, owing to the formation of the III Corps as ordered above, could be extended farther eastwards, by that Corps and by Marwitz's Cavalry Corps, so as to enable a junction to be made with the VII Reserve Corps, which was hurrying up through Laon by forced marches[38] on to the right flank of the Second Army.

The northern bank of the Aisne is very broken and abrupt, the southern bank scarcely less so. The steep, continuous, and well-wooded slopes permitted only a limited and inadequate field of fire on to the enemy's

---

38. From Maubeuge, which, it had been investing, and which surrendered at 6 p.m. on 7th September.

side, a further handicap being the difficulties of observation still prevailing at that time of year. In many places, therefore, the corps abandoned any idea of keeping the Aisne under direct infantry fire, and withdrew to positions on the plateau farther north, where an extensive field of fire was obtainable.

General French, in his despatch of the 8th October, 1914, describes the position of the First Army on the Aisne in the following words:

'The position held by the enemy is a very strong one, either for a delaying action or for a defensive battle. One of its chief military characteristics is that from the high ground on neither side can the top of the plateau on the other side be seen, except for small stretches. This is chiefly due to the woods on the edges of the slopes. Another important point is that all the bridges are under either direct or high-angle artillery fire.

'The tract of country above described, which lies north of the Aisne, is well adapted to concealment, and was so skilfully turned to account by the enemy as to render it impossible to judge the real nature of his opposition to our passage of the river, or to accurately gauge his strength; but I have every reason to conclude that strong rearguards of at least three Army Corps were holding the passages on the early morning of the 13th.'

At about 5 p.m. on the afternoon of the 12th the enemy's infantry, both French and British, was able to cross the Aisne on the front Attichy-Soissons; farther east, however, only a cavalry advance was made.[39] At this period the following Order arrived from the Second Army Commander: 'The enemy forcing back the right flank division has crossed the Vesle and gained the high ground of St. Thierry. The First Army will send as strong a force as possible today in the direction of St. Thierry, towards the rear of the enemy. The remainder of the Army will cover the right flank of this operation. A report will be sent here immediately of what is ordered.' Such an advance by the First Army towards St. Thierry was the less practicable as meanwhile the 13th Infantry Division of the Second Army had had to withdraw from its advanced position in the face of strong enemy forces with its right flank moving on Bourg-et-Comin.

---

39. Von Kluck omits mention of the seizure of the bridge at Venizel by the advanced guard of the 11th Infantry Brigade, 4th Division, in the evening, and its advance to the crest of the plateau beyond.

The First Army could only accept battle in the positions it now occupied, or abandon the strong line of the Aisne and retire farther to the north. The gap between the Second and First Armies would have to be filled by part of the Seventh Army now moving up, whose leading troops were to arrive south of Laon on the 13th. The following message was therefore sent at 8.50 p.m. to the Second Army Commander: 'First Army heavily attacked on front Attichy–Soissons; a battle is expected tomorrow. It is holding the north bank of the Aisne from Attichy to Condé. The left wing can be further prolonged, but any advance towards St. Thierry is out of the question.'

The 12th September marks the beginning of trench-warfare for the First Army on the Aisne. Before provisionally concluding this briefly outlined account of the strategy of the Army, it may be useful to describe the period of transition to position-warfare by means of the decisions made and the orders issued, and thereby to demonstrate how the First Army, by its many days' battle on the Aisne, was called upon to lay the foundation stone for the eventual establishment of the German western front from the Aisne to the Yser. Extracts from a Memorandum, written by the Army Commander to the Second Army Commander, will also be added.

Retrospect

From Army Headquarters, which at that time were close up to the front at Juvigny and behind the artillery positions of the IV Corps, an Army Operation Order was issued on the evening of the 12th, stating that the enemy had succeeded in crossing the Aisne in front of the right wing of the IV Reserve Corps, and further that the VII Corps was retiring from about Braisne towards Vailly. The First Army was to maintain and strengthen its positions. The IV Corps, by arrangement with the IV Reserve Corps, was to support it with heavy artillery from about north-east of Nouvron, and the IX Corps would also support the IV Reserve Corps by enfilade fire from the high ground west of Morsain. It was the duty of the III Corps, co-operating with the II and I Cavalry Corps, to prevent the outflanking of the left wing of the Army. Lepel's Brigade was to attack from Compiègne towards the north bank of the Aisne in the direction of Attichy, as also the 10th *Landwehr* Brigade from Ribecourt. Both brigades were to be affiliated to the IX Corps. The more or less wholesale abandonment of the northern bank of the Aisne, with its many ravines that could be utilized for defence, was to be modified in such manner as the Army Commander thought fit.

In the present condition of infantry armament it would have been advisable to leave a strong covering of modern light machine guns in nooks in the ravines on the slopes of the Aisne during the crossing of the river on the 11th. A few hundreds of these effective weapons would have checked at the outset the attempts of the enemy to cross, and thus gained time in which to strengthen the defence by sending reinforcements where needed. Even a few guns and trench mortars[40] would not have been out of place.

In spite of the measures mentioned above the enterprising enemy forced his way on to the northern bank at Attichy and Vic during the 13th with infantry and artillery, and repeated French attacks were made against the front of the IV Reserve Corps. The IX and IV Reserve Corps were therefore ordered to drive the enemy back on to the ridge immediately above the Aisne. 'The IV Corps will support this attack as strongly as possible, and will send one infantry regiment and a field-artillery brigade[41] from Tartiers to Nouvron to the IV Reserve Corps. The battle-front of the latter corps will be shortened, its right to rest on Hors, north-west of Roche, and its left on the eastern edge of Fontenoy.'

On the evening of the 14th the Army Commander repeated the order to continue reinforcing those positions which had to be held at all costs. If the conditions were favourable, and arrangements were made with the neighbouring corps, counter-attacks might be delivered, reports of which should be made as soon as practicable to Army Headquarters at Juvigny. On the left wing of the Army the III Corps was to attack in a southerly direction from east of Condé, with the VII Reserve Corps and half the XV Corps of the Seventh Army. A mortar battery and a battery of 10 cm. guns under the command of Colonel von Berendt was to be at the disposal of the II Corps to support it and the III Corps.

On the evening of the 15th September Army Headquarters, which had been moved farther back to Vauxaillon were able to state that the First

---

40. These weapons, according to the German General Staff monograph 'Luttich-Namur,' were first used in the attack on Fort Fléron, Liège.
41. Three batteries.

Army had held its position on the whole front. The Seventh Army, with its VII Reserve Corps, had maintained its ground at Bray-en-Laonnois against superior numbers,[42] and east of it the XV and the XII Corps were successfully in action.[43] On the 16th the VII Reserve Corps was to continue its attack, supported by the III Corps. The timely appearance of the VII Reserve Corps, which had come up by forced marches via Laon, and its energetic action, under the leadership of General von Zwehl, at the most endangered part of the Aisne front, will find an important place in the history of this battle of many days, so full of critical situations.

At this time the most welcome news arrived that the IX Reserve Corps of the Seventh Army had reached Pontoise during the afternoon with its advanced guards; on the 16th, co-operating with the IX Corps, it was to drive back the enemy's left wing. The 4th Cavalry Division covered the bridges at Chauny, Condren, and Quierzy in rear of the Army.

If only these three Corps had arrived in the front line of the western wing of the Armies ten days earlier on the Marne!

The reinforcement at last made good the numerical disproportion of the opposing forces.[44] With the conclusion of the many days' Battle of the Aisne came the final transition to position-warfare.[45] It brought with it all the characteristics of the most obstinate siege-warfare with continual

---

42. The British I Corps, after three weeks' heavy campaigning, was hardly superior in numbers to the German VII Reserve Corps, which had done no more than invest Maubeuge.

43. General Von Bülow, however, states that, on account of the critical situation, preparation was made to withdraw to the La Fère line. (See his 'Mein Bericht zur Marne–Schlacht.')

44. This is an interesting admission. The usual Allied calculation has been that, at the Marne, there were forty-six divisions against at least forty-one German. Now Von Kluck tells us that the difference was about three corps – that is, six divisions.

45. During the whole period of the Battle of the Aisne, Von Kluck was under the orders of Von Bülow, but, as the latter states, ignored his orders, so that he had eventually to appeal to the Supreme Command to prevent Von Kluck from repeating on the Aisne the manoeuvre of attacking westwards, leaving a gap between First and Second Armies like that which was the cause of the defeat on the Marne.

alternation of rest and hard fighting, all under an incessant artillery fire. The vast amount of work required for constructing the positions in the numberless sectors of the front, supported by *points d'appui* both for defence and counter-attack; the constant pulling out of mobile reserves, especially after the IV and II Corps had been sent elsewhere; the building of shelters and dug-outs above and below ground for man and horse; the repair of worn-out roads; far-reaching measures for the care of the health of the troops and for their food-supply; keeping the front line up to strength and replenishing the ammunition depots; provision of fortress artillery; regulating the means of communication and the system of traffic behind the front – all these now began, and countless other important tasks as well.

With the growth in the strength of the field works, corps commanders, in the interests of the welfare of their troops, introduced a regular system of reliefs for the men on outpost fighting in the front line. Under the far-seeing leadership of the General Commanding the Pioneers, Generalleutnant Telle, the excellent and indefatigable Pioneers gave every assistance to the infantry in their digging, and with the utmost devotion carried out the most dangerous operations above and below ground in trench-warfare, and in mining operations later on. Pioneer depots grew, as it were, out of the ground. The artillery with its fully matured war experience supported the infantry as much as possible, in spite of its own shortness of ammunition, until that crisis was also overcome, and the Army was able to undertake extensive operations at Bailly and Soissons. The lines of communications, which, as before, were under Generalleutnant von Bertrab, increased their efficiency to the highest pitch.

At last, when the Battle of the Aisne was over, circumstances permitted a richly deserved rest and occasional recreation to be given to the corps of the First Army, to those sons of Holstein, of the Marches of Brandenburg, of Pomerania, Saxony, and Schleswig, who had never failed in their duty. In the meantime Marwitz's horsemen, under their celebrated leaders, hastened northwards, where for years armies from Lorraine anchored the northern wing of the German Western Armies firmly in that blood-soaked soil from Artois and Flanders to the coast. This was the basis for a successful campaign in the East, and a primary condition for the inevitable future offensive against the enemies in the West.

From the time of its departure from the concentration area between the Rhine and the western frontier of Germany, north of Aix-la-Chapelle, up till its arrival on the Grand Morin, east of Paris, the First Army, its points, advanced guards and main bodies, fighting on the majority of days, had covered in about thirty days a distance of over 312 miles, and, if the distance back to the Aisne is added, far over 375 miles, in varying order of battle and without a rest-day.

The names of its leaders, Generals Gronau, Kuhl, Linsingen, Lochow, Marwitz, Sixt von Armin, and Quast, came brilliantly to the front, and the experience gained by them in commanding such unsurpassed troops brought them during the following years to the command of Armies and Army Groups, and to the leading positions on the decisive battle-fronts.

During the September fighting far the greater part of the success, tactically speaking, fell to the German Western Army, but strategically the enemy gained the upper hand, since he was able to compel the German Supreme Command to arrange a completely fresh grouping of the Western Army at another part of the line.

It is clear that the gallant Sixth French Army under Maunoury, ordered by General Gallieni on the 4th September to attack the First Army, had, together with the Army of Sir John French, a comparatively simple operation to perform, whereas the corps of the First Army were called upon to carry out one which strained their capacity of manoeuvre to the utmost, and whose complications and difficulties were such as have seldom been met with in the history of great wars.

Some Accidents of War

Owing to some unfortunate circumstances which have not been cleared up, the control of the Supreme Command over the western wing Armies was by no means firm. This may be seen both from the description of the September fighting on the German western wing in the records and from the following report to the Second Army Commander sent from Vauxaillon on the 16th September. Its opening sentences show clearly the dangers from which the First Army escaped by a timely withdrawal after its isolated attack against Maunoury's Army:

'From the wireless message from the Supreme Command, sent from Luxemburg at 11.55 p.m. on the 15th September, to the Second Army

Commander, it is clear that an order must have been given at an earlier-period for the First Army "to guard against surprise on its right flank by moving in a clearly defined echelon formation." Another Supreme Command Order must also have been issued on the 14th, according to which "the First Army is to avoid any dangerous enemy operation against its flank by withdrawing due northwards." Neither of these Orders arrived here, and their existence only became known the morning after through the above-mentioned wireless message.

'Until now the First Army has considered its duty to consist in holding the Aisne position in order to cover the flank of the Armies. The right flank has been withdrawn to the vicinity of Cuts, south of Noyon, the left flank remains at and north-east of Vailly. According to instructions received from the Second Army Commander, the left wing of the First Army was to attack in the direction of Fismes with as strong a force as possible, to exploit the success of the left wing of the Second Army. The III Corps, at the urgent request of the Seventh Army, and in accordance with the order of the Second Army Commander, therefore attacked today on the front Condé-Vailly and north-east of it, in support of the VII Reserve Corps.

'The enemy is in strength on the whole front of the First Army, and makes intermittent attacks in various places. The right wing of the Army, the IX Corps, which had been drawn back, was yesterday threatened by an enveloping attack from about Compiègne on Cuts. As the IX Reserve Corps, belonging to the Seventh Army, has already been sent by that Army to Noyon, there is a possibility of preventing the enveloping movement and forcing the enemy back again.

'The IX Corps and IX Reserve Corps are, therefore, to attack today and drive back the enemy, but the right flank will be withdrawn again afterwards, and the IX Reserve Corps, so far as it is at the disposal of the First Army, will be echeloned back north of the Aisne.

'If the absence of any clear report by First Army Headquarters regarding the danger threatening the right flank of the Armies has given rise to dissatisfaction, it must be stated that, unfortunately, nothing in the nature of a clear report could be obtained. Both cavalry and air reconnaissances have failed during the past few days. It appears, however, that only strong French cavalry is advancing north of the Oise, strength from two to three divisions. The strong column of all arms, previously reported, is marching from Compiègne on Noyon. The II Cavalry Corps has been ordered to march towards Chauny.

'I request a decision as to whether the centre of the Army is to hold the Aisne line or not. An offensive of the left wing towards Fismes, or even merely an energetic support of the right wing of the Seventh Army, is only possible if the line of the Aisne is held. A withdrawal of the First Army, "in a direction due north," in face of the enemy immediately opposed to it, would place the Seventh and Second Armies in an exceptionally dangerous situation. The strong forces of the enemy, which until now have been held by the First Army, would gain a free hand for further operations.

'Taking everything into consideration, I think it preferable for the First Army to hold on to the Aisne position for the time being, with its left flank supporting the Seventh Army, and its right wing bent back, with the IX Reserve Corps echeloned north of the Oise, as soon as the threatened enveloping attack has been repulsed. If a more extensive echelon formation is ordered, it can only be carried out by fresh forces, or else by giving up the line of the Aisne, in which case it should be borne in mind that strong enemy forces are close up to the First Army on the whole of its front; and if the idea of withdrawing due north is persisted in, it cannot be combined with an offensive of the left wing, or with the duty of protecting the flank of the Seventh and Second Armies.

'(*Signed*) Von Kluck.'

The temporary subordination of Armies to the commander of a neighbouring Army will seldom be found to diminish or terminate a strategical or high tactical crisis, and the better course in such a case would have been for the Supreme Command to intervene, and place the three wing Armies under one, or the senior, Commander, and simultaneously to relieve him of the command of his own Army. If such a procedure, which was made use of later during the war, was not regarded as desirable with large modern Armies, another course, worthy of recommendation, would have been to place the Chief of the General Staff in temporary command of the right wing Armies in the area Noyon–Reims, under His Majesty's orders. The fortune of war is on the side of thorough measures.

With the establishment of the First Army on the high ground along the northern bank of the Aisne an oppressively heavy burden, both in a strategic and tactical sense, was removed from the shoulders of its famous corps and their capable commanders of all grades. The heroic troops could look back on their long campaign with memories full of glory, toil, and devotion to duty against enemies worthy of their steel; they could think, not without emotion, of the sufferings of their wounded comrades, and of those left behind on the numerous battlefields, who had given their lives for the Emperor, for the Country, and for Honour. Their high courage and devotion to duty remains steadfast. To work for victory in happy combination one with another was the thought of all. No one set value on individual glory.

Appendix

Order of Battle of the First Army, 1914

Army Troops

Siege Units:
Staff 1st Guard Foot Artillery.
General of Pioneers attached to Army
Staff:
  Pioneer Regt. 18 (2 battns.). (At
    disposal of I Army Corps until
    eighth day of mobilization.)
  Pioneer Siege Train (2 Park coys.).
  Searchlight Section (from 1.10.14).

Telegraph and Air Force Units:
Army Telegraph Sections I, III.
Lines of Communication Telephone
  Detachment.
Wireless Command 1.
Wireless Station 5 (III).
Wireless Station 20.
Balloon Section 1.
Aeroplane Section 12.

Lines of Communication Units:
Lines of Communication Inspection II.
  With Lines of Communication
  Units of II, III, and IV Army
  Corps and 2nd Lines of
  Communication Units of III and
  IV Army Corps.

Motor Transport Units:
O.C. Motor Transport Train 1.
L. of C. Motor Columns 1–4.
L. of C. Motor Columns 25–26.
L. of C. Motor Columns 47–50.

L. of C. Motor Columns 22–24.
L. of C. Motor Columns 35–36
L. of C. Motor Columns 45–46.
L. of C. Motor Columns 38.
L. of C. Motor Park 1.

Motor Transport Units:
L. of C. Aircraft Park 1.

*Lines of Communication Ammunition
Columns:*
  Nos. 5 and 6 of II Army Corps.
  Nos. 7, 8. 47 of III Army Corps.
  Nos. 9, 10, 49 of IV Army Corps.

Lines of Communication Transport Columns:
  Nos. 1–4 of II Army Corps.
  Nos. 1–4 of III Army Corps.
  Nos. 1–4 of IV Army Corps.

Reserve Supply Columns:
  Nos. 1–3 II.
  Nos. 4–6 II.
  Nos. 1–3 IV.
  Nos. 4–6 IV.
  Nos. 1–3 IX.

1st Army Reserve Ammunition, Stores, Gas:
  Ammunition Trains (loaded trucks):
    Infantry 1–2 II; 6, 38 III.
  Field Artillery:
    Howitzer 5–8 II; 11, 16 III; 22, 26
      IV.
    Gun 3 III; 6 IV.

Foot Artillery:
Heavy Field Howitzer and Heavy Gun 2 V.; 3 III.; 4 IV.
Stores and Explosive Reserve (loaded railway trucks) 1 III.
Gas Reserve (attached to Stores and Explosives) 1 VIII.
Transport Stores (two sections, each with eight days' Army supply in Lines of Communication Motor Park).

Note: Demands for further supplies will be sent as follows – for Ammunition and Stores to Chief of Field Ammunition Department; for Personnel, Vehicles, Spare Parts, etc., for motors and transport stores of all kinds to the Stationary Motor Department 1 VII. Düsseldorf; for Gas to the Field Balloon Section, Stationary Aircraft Troops Inspection.

Corps
Total troops

Field and Reserve	124 battalions	32 squadrons	96 batteries, 12 Pioneer Coys.
Landwehr	18 battalions	3 squadrons	0 batteries.
Landsturrn	0 battalions	0 battalions	2 battalions

Note: Jäger battalions 3 III and 4 IV were temporarily detailed to 2nd Division of II Cavalry Corps.

III CORPS
(25 battalions, 6 squadrons, 24 batteries, 4 Pioneer Coys.)

5th Division:
9th Infantry Brigade:
8th Regt.
48th Regt.
10th Infantry Brigade:
12th Regt.
52nd Regt.
(Each regiment of 3 battalions and a machine-gun company.)
3rd Jäger Battn.
3rd Hussars (3 squadrons).
5th Field Artillery Brigade:
18th Field Artillery Regt:
I. Abteilung (3 batteries and light ammunition column.)
II. Abteilung (howitzers).
54th Field Artillery Regt:

I. Abteilung.
II. Abteilung
Engineers:
1st Coy. 3rd Pioneer Battn.
5th Divisional Bridging Train.
Medical:
1st and 3rd Medical Coys.

6th Division:
11th Infantry Brigade:
20th Regt.
35th Regt.
12th Infantry Brigade:
24th Regt.
64th Regt.
(Each regiment of 3 battalions and a machine-gun company.)
3rd Hussars (Regimental Staff and 3 squadrons).
6th Field Artillery Brigade:
3rd Field Artillery Regt:

I Abteilung (3 batteries and light ammunition column).

II Abteilung (3 batteries and light ammunition column).

39th Artillery Regt:

I Abteilung.

II Abteilung (howitzers).

Engineers:

2nd Coy. 3rd Pioneer Battn.

3rd Coy. 3rd Pioneer Battn.

6th Divisional Bridging Train.

Medical:

2nd Medical Coy.

Corps Troops:

Searchlight Section, 3rd Pioneer Battn.

3rd Telephone Section.

7th Aeroplane Section.

1st Battn. 2nd Guard Foot Artillery Regt. (4 companies and light ammunition column).

Ammunition Columns:

No. I. Infantry 1 and 2.

Artillery 1, 2, 3, 4 (howitzer).

Ammunition Columns:

No. II Infantry 3 and 4.

Artillery 5, 6, 7, 8 (howitzer); 9 (howitzer).

Foot Artillery 1–8.

Trains:

No. I   Field Hospitals 1–6.

Supply Columns 1–3.

Transport Columns 1–3

Horse Depot 1.

No. II Field Hospitals 7–12.

Supply Columns 4–6.

Transport Columns 4–7.

Horse Depot 2.

Corps Bridging Train 3.

Field Bakery Columns 1, 2.

Landwehr:

11th Brigade.:

20th Regt., 3 battalions.

35th Regt., 3 battalions.

1st Squadron Guard Landwehr.

2nd Landsturm Battery III Corps.*

10th Brigade:

12th Regt., 3 battalions.

52nd Regt., 3 battalions.

1st Squadron Landwehr.

1st Landsturm Battery III Corps.*

27th Brigade:

53rd Regt., 3 battalions.

55th Regt., 3 battalions.

2nd Squadron Landwehr. (This brigade, until sixteenth day of mobilization, was at disposal of VII Army Corps for railway protection.)

IV CORPS

(25 battalions, 6 squadrons, 24 batteries, 4 Pioneer Coys.)

7th Division:

13th Infantry Brigade:

26th Regt.

66th Regt.

14th Infantry Brigade:

27th Regt.

165th Regt.

(Each regiment of 3 battalions and a machine-gun company.)

10th Hussars (Staff and 3 squadrons).

7th Field Artillery Brigade:

4th Field Artillery Regt.:

I   Abteilung (3 batteries and light ammunition column).

II Abteilung (howitzer).

* Attached

40th Field Artillery Regt.:
  I   Abteilung.
  II Abteilung.
Engineers :
  1st Coy. 4th Pioneer Battn.
  7th Divisional Bridging Train.
Medical:
  1st and 3rd Medical Coys.

8th Division :
  15th Infantry Brigade:
    36th Regt.
    93rd Regt.
    4th Jäger Battn.
  16th Infantry Brigade:
    72nd Regt.
    153rd Regt.
    (Each regiment of 3 battalions and 1
    machine-gun company.)
  10th Hussars (3 squadrons).
  8th Field Artillery Brigade:
    74th Artillery Regt.:
      I Abteilung (3 batteries and light
      ammunition column).
      II Abteilung.
    75th Artillery Regt.:
      I Abteilung.
      II Abteilung (howitzer).
  Engineers:
    2nd and 3rd Coys. 4th Pioneer
    Battn.
    8th Divisional Bridging Train.
  Medical:
    2nd Medical Coy.

Corps Troops:
  Searchlight Section 4th Pioneer Battn.
  4th Telephone Section.
  9th Aeroplane Section.
  1st Battn. 4th Foot Artillery Regt.
  (4 companies and light ammunition
  column).

Ammunition Columns:
  No. 1.   Infantry 1 and 2.
           Artillery 1, 2, 3, and 4
           (howitzer).
  No II   Infantry 3 and 4.
           Artillery 5, 6, 7, 8
           (howitzer), and 9
           (howitzer).
  Foot Artillery 1–8.
Trains:
  No. I   Field Hospitals 1–6.
           Supply Columns 1–3.
           Transport Columns 1-3.
           Horse Depot 1.
  No. II   Field Hospitals 7–12.
           Supply Columns 4–6.
           Transport Columns 4–7.
           Horse Depot 2.
  Corps Bridging Train 4.
  Field Bakery Columns 1 and 2.

IV RESERVE CORPS
(25 battalions, 6 squadrons, 12 batteries.)

7th Reserve Division:
  13th Reserve Infantry Brigade:
    27th Regt. (3 battalions and
    M.G. Coy).
    36th Regt. (3 battalions).
  14th Reserve Infantry Brigade:
    66th Regt. (3 battalions).
    72nd Regt. (3 battalions and M.G.
    Coy.).
  4th Reserve Jäger Battn.
  1st Reserve Heavy Cavalry Regt.
  7th Reserve Field Artillery Regt.
    I   Abteilung (3 batteries and light
        ammunition column).
    II Abteilung (3 batteries and light
        ammunition column).
  Engineers:
    4th Coy. 4th Pioneer Battn.
    7th Reserve Divisional Bridging
    Train.

Medical:
   4th Reserve Medical Coy.

22nd Reserve Division:
   43rd Reserve Infantry Brigade:
      71st Regt. (3 battalions).
      94th Regt. (2 battalions and M.G.
      Coy.).
      11th Reserve Jäger Battn.
   44th Reserve Infantry Brigade:
      32nd Regt. (3 battalions).
      82nd Regt. (3 battalions and M.G.
      Coy.).
   1st Reserve Jäger Mounted Regt.
   22nd Reserve Field Artillery Regt.
      I   Abteilung (3 batteries and light
          ammunition column).
      II Abteilung (3 batteries and light
          ammunition column.
   Engineers :
      1st Reserve Coy. 4th Pioneer Battn.
      2nd Reserve Coy. 4th Pioneer
      Battn.
      22nd Reserve Divisional Bridging
      Train.
   Medical:
      11th Reserve Medical Coy.
   Engineers:
      4th Reserve Telephone Section.
   Ammunition Columns :
      7th Reserve Ammunition Column:
         Infantry Sections 11 and 12.
         Artillery Sections 14, 15, and
         40.
      22nd Reserve Ammunition Column:
         Infantry Sections 25 and 26.
         Artillery Sections 35 and 36.
   Trains:
      7th Reserve Train:
         Field Hospitals 21–23.
         Supply Columns 11 and 12.
         Transport Columns 10 and 11.

22nd Reserve Train:
   Field Hospitals 24, 49, 50.
   Transport Columns 3, 12, 31, 32.
Field Bakery Columns 6 and 13.

II CORPS
(24 Battalions, 6 squadrons, 24 batteries, 4
Pioneer Coys.)

3rd Division:
   5th Infantry Brigade:
      2nd Regt.
      9th Regt.
   6th Infantry Brigade:
      34th Regt.
      42nd Regt.
      (Each regiment of 3 battalions and 1
         machine-gun company.)
   3rd Dragoons.
   3rd Field Artillery Brigade:
      2nd Field Artillery Regt.:
         I   Abteilung (3 batteries and
             light ammunition column.)
         II Abteilung.
      38th Field Artillery Regt.:
         I   Abteilung.
         II Abteilung (howitzer).
   Engineers:
      1st Coy. 2nd Pioneer Battn.
      3rd Divisional Bridging Train.
   Medical:
      1st and 3rd Medical Coys.

4th Division:
   7th Infantry Brigade:
      14th Regt.
      149 Regt.
   8th Infantry Brigade:
      49th Regt.
      140th Regt.
      (Each regiment of 3 battalions and 1
         machine-gun company.)

12th Dragoons.
4th Field Artillery Brigade:
   17th Field Artillery Regt.:
     I Abteilung (3 batteries and
       light ammunition column).
     II Abteilung (howitzer).
   53rd Field Artillery Regt.:
     I Abteilung.
     II Abteilung.
Engineers:
   2nd and 3rd Coys. 2nd Pioneer
   Battn.
   4th Divisional Bridging Train.
Medical:
   2nd Medical Coy.

Corps Troops:
   Searchlight Section 2nd Pioneer Battn.
   2nd Telephone Section.
   30th Aeroplane Section (from 1st July,
     1914, onwards).
   1st Battn. 15th Foot Artillery Regt.
     (4 companies and light ammunition
     column).
   Ammunition Columns:
     No. I Infantry 1 and 2.
       Artillery 1, 2, 3, and 4 (howitzer).
     No. II Infantry 3 and 4.
       Artillery 5, 6, 7, 8 (howitzer), and
         9 (howitzer).
     Foot Artillery 1–8.
     No. I Field Hospitals 1–6.
     Supply Columns 1–3.
     Transport Columns 1–3.
     Horse Depot 1.
     No. II Field Hospitals 7–12.
     No. II Supply Columns 4–6.
     Transport Columns 7.
     Horse Depot 2.
     Corps Bridging Train 2.
     Field Bakery Columns 1 and 2

III RESERVE CORPS
(25 battalions, 6 squadrons, 12 batteries.)

5th Reserve Division:
   9th Reserve Infantry Brigade:
     8th Regt.
     48th Regt.
   10th Reserve Infantry Brigade:
     12th Regt.
     52nd Regt.
       (Each regiment of 3 battalions and
       a machine-gun company.)
   3rd Reserve Jäger Battn.
   2nd Reserve Dragoons.
   5th Reserve Field Artillery Regt.:
     I Abteilung (3 batteries and light
       ammunition column).
     II Abteilung.
   Engineers :
     4th Coy. 3rd Pioneer Battn.
     5th Reserve Divisional Bridging
       Train.
   Medical:
     3rd Reserve Medical Coy.

6th Reserve Division:
   11th Reserve Infantry Brigade:
     20th Regt. (3 battalions and M.G.
       Coy.).
     24th Regt. (3 battalions and M.G.
       Coy.).
   12th Reserve Infantry Brigade:
     26th Regt. (3 battalions).
     35th Regt. (3 battalions and M.G.
       Coy.).
   3rd Reserve Uhlans.
   6th Reserve Field Artillery Regt:
     I Abteilung (3 batteries and light
       ammunition column).
     II Abteilung.
   Engineers:
     1st and 2nd Coys. 3rd Reserve
       Pioneer Battn.

6th Reserve Divisional Bridging
Train.
Medical:
16th Reserve Medical Coy.

Corps Troops:
Engineers:
3rd Reserve Telephone Section.
Ammunition Columns:
5th Reserve Ammunition Column:
Infantry Reserve Sections 9 and
10.
Artillery Reserve Sections 2, 11,
and 12.
6th Reserve Ammunition Column:
Infantry Reserve Sections 27 and
41.
Artillery Reserve Sections 13 and
46.
Trains:
5th Reserve Train:
Field Hospital Reserve Sections
18, 19, and 20.
Transport Reserve Sections 7, 8,
and 9.
6th Reserve Train:
Field Hospital Reserve Sections
64, 65, and 66.
Transport Reserve Sections 46,
47, 48, and 49.
Field Bakery Reserve Columns 5
and 16.

IX CORPS
(25 battalions, 6 squadrons, 24 batteries, 4
Pioneer Coys.)

17th Division:
33rd Infantry Brigade:
75th Regt.
76th Regt.
34th Infantry Brigade:
89th Regt.

90th Regt.
(Each regiment of 3 battalions and 1
machine-gun company.)
3 Cavalry squadrons.
17th Field Artillery Brigade:
24th Field Artillery Regt.:
I Abteilung (3 batteries and
light ammunition column).
II Abteilung.
60th Field Artillery Regt.:
I Abteilung.
II Abteilung (howitzers).
Engineers:
2nd Coy. 9th Pioneer Battn.
Divisional Bridging Train.
Medical:
1 Medical Coy.

18th Division:
35th Infantry Brigade:
84th Regt.
86th Regt.
36th Infantry Brigade:
31st Regt.
85th Regt.
(Each regiment of 3 battalions and 1
machine-gun company.)
9th Jäger Battn.
3 Cavalry Squadrons.
18th Field Artillery Brigade:
9th Artillery Regt.
I Abteilung (3 batteries and
light ammunition column).
II Abteilung.
45th Field Artillery Regt.
I Abteilung.
II Abteilung (howitzers)
Engineers:
1st Coy. 9th Pioneer Battn.
Divisional Bridging Train.
Medical:
3rd Medical Coy.

Corps Troops:
    Searchlight Section 4th Pioneer Battn.
    Telephone Section.
    Aeroplane Section.
    1st Battn. 20th Foot Artillery Regt.
        (4 companies and light ammunition
        column).
    Ammunition Columns:
      No. I Infantry 1 and 2.
        Artillery 1, 2, 3, and 4.
      No. II Infantry 1 and 2.
        Artillery 1, 2, 3, 4, and 5.

Ammunition Columns:
    Foot Artillery 1–8.
Trains:
    No. I Field Hospitals 1–6.
      Supply Columns 1–3.
      Transport Columns 1–3.
      Horse Depot 1.
    No. II Field Hospitals 1–6.
      Supply Columns 1–3.
      Transport Columns 1–4.
      Horse Depot 2.
Corps Bridging Train 9.
Field Bakery Columns 1 and 2.

Bibliography

Secret and other papers of the First Army Commander from 9th August to 15th September, 1914.

Memorandum by the Chief of the General Staff of the First Army on the operations during the same period, dated 29th May, 1915.

Despatches of Sir John French of 1914.

Die Schlachten an der Marne vom 6 bis 12 September, 1914. Mittler und Sohn, 1916. Author anonymous.

Hermann Stegemann. Der Krieg. First volume, 1917.

Colonel K. Egli. Zwei Jahre Weltkrieg. August, 1914, to August, 1916.

Daily notes of the First Army Commander.

Die Marneschlacht. Professor Dr. Walter Kolbe. Rostock, 1917.

Strategisches aus dem Weltkrieg. V. Nordenswan, Major-General in the Swedish Army.

Stegemann's Weltkrieg und die Marneschlacht. Karl Bleibtreu.

Der Feldzug, 1914. Die Marneschlacht. Original in French by Major Gedel. 1916.

La Victoire de la Marne. Louis Madelin, in the *Revue des deux mondes*. September, 1916.

L'Illustration of 11th September, 1915.

Je sais tout. *Magasin de l'activité et de l'energ-ie nationales*. 15th September, 1917.

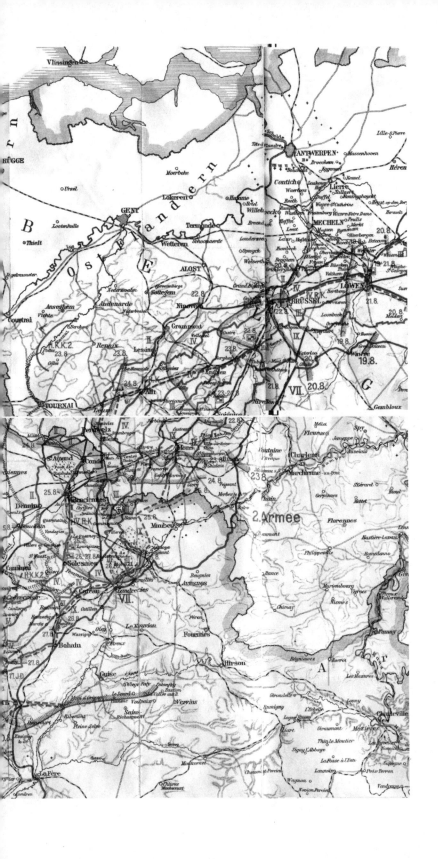

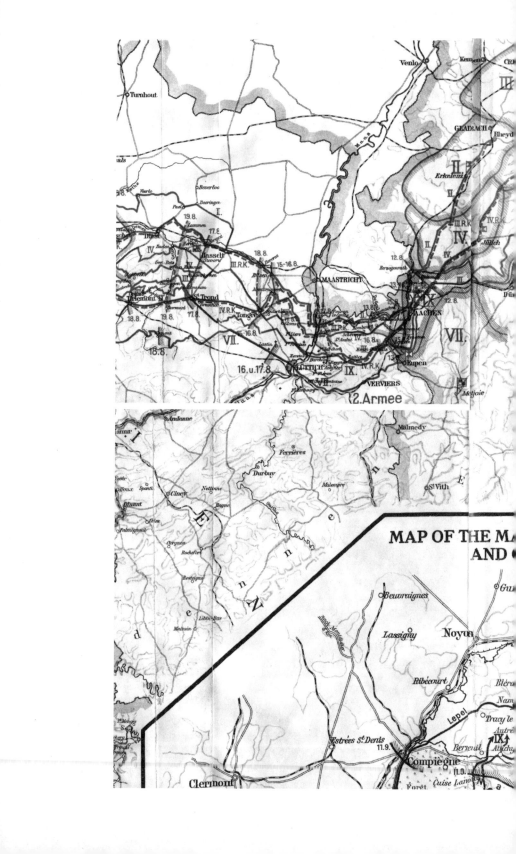

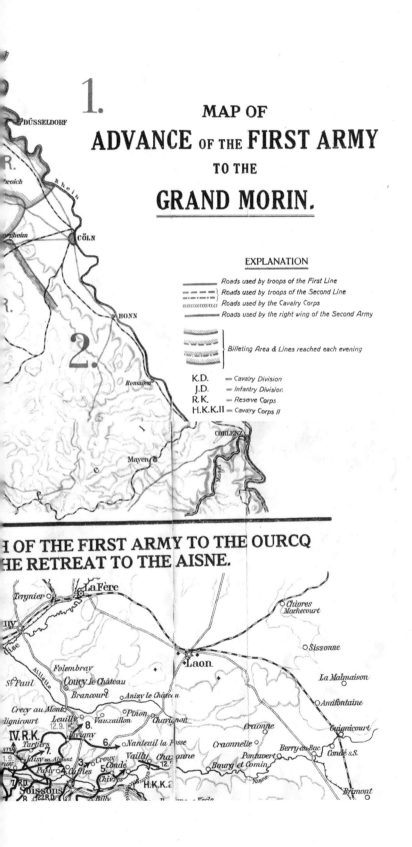

1.
MAP OF
ADVANCE OF THE FIRST ARMY
TO THE
GRAND MORIN.

EXPLANATION

———————— Roads used by troops of the First Line
= = = = = Roads used by troops of the Second Line
《《《《《《《《《 Roads used by the Cavalry Corps
———————— Roads used by the right wing of the Second Army

Billeting Area & Lines reached each evening

K.D. = Cavalry Division
J.D. = Infantry Division
R.K. = Reserve Corps
H.K.K.II = Cavalry Corps II

DÜSSELDORF

R.

broich

Rhein

rgheim

CÖLN

R.

BONN

2.

Remagen

COBLENZ

Mayen

Mosel

I OF THE FIRST ARMY TO THE OURCQ
HE RETREAT TO THE AISNE.

La Fère
Terpnier

Chivres
Machecourt

IIY

Oise

Sissonne

Folembray
St Paul
Coucy le Château
Aillette
Brancourt
Anizy le Château
Crecy au Mont
lignicourt
Leuilly
Vauxaillon
Chavignon
8.
12.9.
avigny
6.
Tartiers
Nanteuil la Fosse
7.
1.9.
nov.
issy en Aisont
3.
Crouy
Vailly
Chavonne
12.
Pasly
Condé
Chivres
7.R.D.
SOISSONS
R
22.R.D.
Billy
H.K.K.2

Laon

La Malmaison

Amifontaine

Pinon

Craonne

Grignicourt

Craonnelle
Pontavert
Berry au Bac
Condé s.S.
Bourg et Comin

Brimont

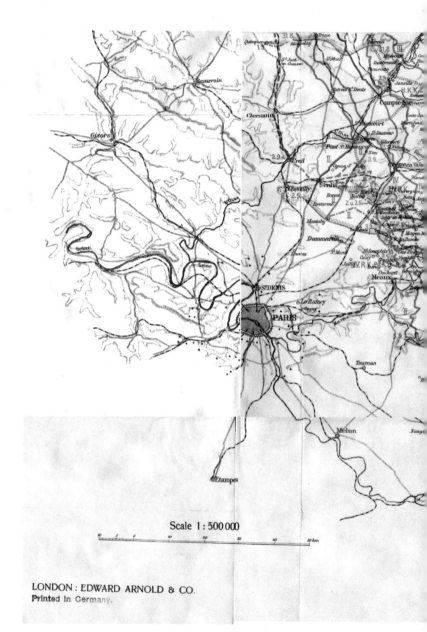

Scale 1 : 500 000

LONDON : EDWARD ARNOLD & CO.
Printed in Germany.

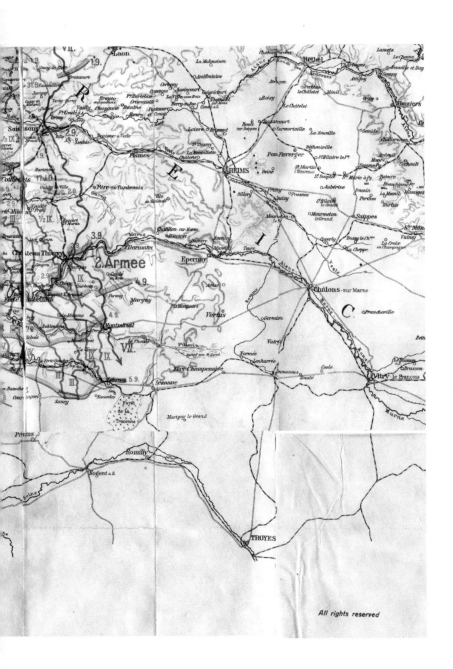

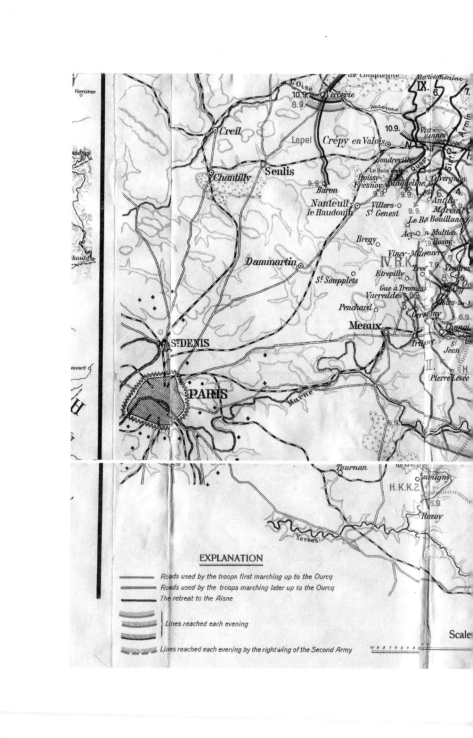

EXPLANATION

Roads used by the troops first marching up to the Ourcq
Roads used by the troops marching later up to the Ourcq
The retreat to the Aisne

Lines reached each evening

Lines reached each evening by the right wing of the Second Army

Scale

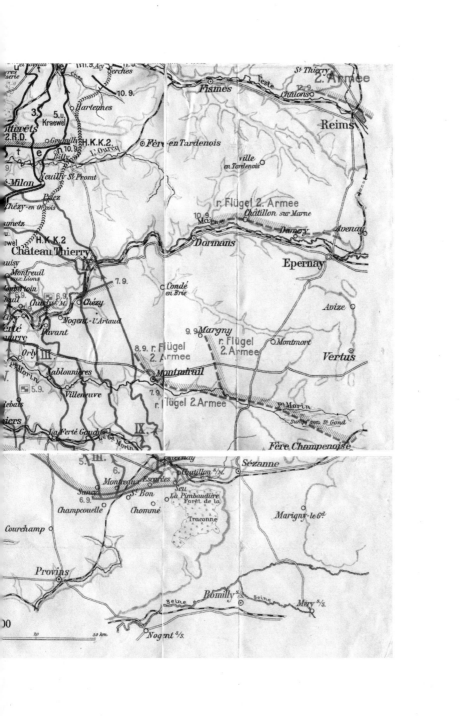